NAHC

Wild Game Cookbook

designed and edited by

Mark LaBarbera
Valarie Waldron
Jane Obern

reviewed by
Executive Chef Scott Ekenberg

Published by the North American Hunting Club, Inc.,
Minneapolis, MN 55435

Address reprint requests and
orders for additional books to:

NAHC Cookbook Editor
Post Office Box 35557
Minneapolis, MN 55435

CONTENTS

WHY THIS ALL-NEW COOKBOOK?

Paul S. Burke, Jr.

Just when I thought we had explored every conceivable concoction for preparing wild game meat; just when I thought we had shared every recipe from muskrat and moose to mountain goat and goose, the North American Hunting Club staff came up with some great new ideas.

If you feel like you're already up to your cartridge belts in cookbooks, rest assured that this one is likely to be the most valuable addition yet to your kitchen.

This All-New "NAHC Wild Game Cookbook" has more recipes than any other cookbook you've ever received from the Club. You're getting two years' worth of new recipes all in this one book, and you're getting it for the price of only one book.

The all-time best meals you'll ever prepare are likely to come from two new sections created especially for you and other NAHC members. The first section comes from professional big game guides and their camp cooks. We think now we've captured some of their secrets to help make you an even better wild game cook.

Then we took the cookbook one giant step forward to make it the most complete book possible and to bring you from campfires to microwaves. To be honest with you, we stumbled upon our own NAHC Charter Member celebrity during our Jamboree in Reno, Nevada. Here she was, an avid hunter and published cookbook author. Charter Member Paula Del Giudice willingly shares 40 of her favorite wild game recipes with you and other NAHC members in this book. This is one of the few places where you can find microwave oven recipes designed exclusively for wild game. Paula's proven recipes are perfect for anyone who hunts game and cooks with a microwave.

But Paula doesn't stop there. In this NAHC cookbook she shows you how to convert your microwave game recipes for use in your conventional oven. So even if you don't have a microwave, you are treated to 40 great game meals.

The microwave section and the camp cook section are enough to fill most cookbooks, but we're not stopping there. We're going the extra mile for you. In this cookbook you'll be pleased to find three more valuable sections.

First, you'll receive more than 70 of the best recipes for big and small game, upland birds, waterfowl and varmints handpicked from those submitted by your fellow members from across the country. With all types of game, varieties of spices and styles of cooking, you'll find it's a learning experience to sample these great recipes.

Second, you'll find we've added about a dozen savory recipes from the hunting executives at some of the world's well-known outdoor companies. While you're waiting for their mouth-watering recipes to cook, you can sit down with your "NAHC Wild Game Cookbook" and read the interesting histories of their companies.

To top it all off your cookbook includes a selection of Executive Chef Scott Ekenberg's "Favorite Wild Game Meals". Scott, who is a Charter Member of the Club, shares full menus so you can have great recipes at your fingertips for any occasion, from a romantic evening for two to a dinner party for a group of important friends and relatives.

Unlike other cookbooks, the "NAHC Wild Game Cookbook" gives you all of this and puts it in an easy-to-follow format that has proven itself time and again in hunter's kitchens across the country. Enjoy it.

MICRO YOUR GAME!

Paula with fellow NAHC'ers at our National Jamboree.

Paula Del Giudice (pronounced ga-deece), the 28-year-old NAHC Charter Member who contributed this entire Microwave Game Cooking section, deserves the gratitude of every NAHC member, like you, who uses this All-New "NAHC Wild Game Cookbook". She worked on these recipes, developed and perfected them, before so generously contributing them for all of her fellow members to enjoy.

If you have a microwave oven, this section fills the gap left by other, less-complete cookbooks. If you don't have a microwave, these recipes can easily be converted for use in your regular oven. Simply set the oven at 350 degrees and cook the meat three times as long as listed for microwave cooking. It's that easy — now that Paula has told us how to do it!

Paula possesses an insuppressible passion for the outdoors, and it extends into the kitchen. She is an active member of the Outdoor Writers Association of America and Founder/President of the Southwest Outdoor Writers Association. She is a member of sporting clubs, associations, federations and foundations, plus takes an active role in politics to support outdoor causes. Paula's outdoor experience developed even further during her years as Senior Editor of a shotgunning magazine and State Editor of two regional publications for sportsmen.

Her outdoor writing appears in national magazines, and now she has completed a book, the "Microwave Game and Fish Cookbook," available for $12.95. If you'd like an autographed copy, add on $2.50 for postage and handling, tell her who it's for and order directly from Paula, (3031 Chavez Dr., Dept. NAH, Reno, NV 89502).

MICROWAVE
RECIPES

MOOSE SAUERBRATEN

Serves: 6

- 1 3-3½ lbs. moose chuck roast
- 2 T. oil
- ¾ cup gingersnaps, crushed
- 2 tsp. sugar

Marinade:

1 onion, sliced	6 cloves
2 bay leaves	1 cup cider vinegar
15 peppercorns	½ cup boiling water

Place roast in bowl with marinade ingredients. Cover tightly and refrigerate for at least three days. Turn the roast twice a day. Be careful not to pierce the meat when turning. Drain the meat, reserving marinade. Heat oil in skillet and brown the roast on all sides. Remove meat to a glass baking dish. Add marinade, insert temperature probe and micro on 60 percent until temperature reaches 130 to 140 degrees. Remove meat and onions and cover with foil. Strain the liquid in casserole and measure it. Add water if necessary to bring the total of liquid to two cups. Pour back into the casserole and micro on high for three to four minutes. Stir the gingersnaps and sugar into the liquid. Micro on high for two to three minutes. Serve meat and onions on a platter with the gravy.

SWEET AND SOUR ANTELOPE

Serves: 6

  1 **lb. antelope round steak, cut into thin strips**
1¾ **cups water**
  1 **tsp. salt**
  ¼ **cup soy sauce**
  1 **clove garlic**
  ⅓ **cup sugar**
  ¼ **cup cornstarch**
  ¼ **cup cider vinegar**
  ⅓ **cup pineapple juice**
  ¼ **tsp. ginger**
  ¾ **cup pineapple chunks**
  1 **bell pepper, cut into 1-inch chunks**
     sesame seeds
     rice

Place antelope strips, water, salt, soy sauce and garlic in a 2-quart saucepan. Micro on high until at a boil, approximately five minutes. Micro on simmer or medium until meat is just barely cooked, about 12 to 15 minutes. Discard garlic. Drain the broth through a coffee filter or cheesecloth to remove meat drippings. Set meat aside and reserve broth. In a saucepan, blend the sugar, cornstarch, vinegar, pineapple juice and ginger until smooth. Gradually stir in meat broth. Cook on high until sauce is thick and transparent, stopping and stirring every two minutes until done, approximately six to eight minutes. Combine the sauce with antelope, pineapple chunks, sesame seeds and bell pepper. Let sit for several minutes, covered, to finish cooking. Stir. Serve over bed of rice.

GARDEN FRESH GUMBO

Serves: 8-10

- 2 lbs. antelope round steak or stew meat, cut into bite-sized pieces
- 1 onion, chopped
- 2 stalks celery, chopped
- 3 sprigs parsley, chopped
- 1 clove garlic, chopped
- 1 48 oz. can tomato juice
- 3 T. oil
- 1 cup corn
- 2 cups water
  salt and pepper
- 3 carrots, chopped
- 1 zucchini, chopped
- 1 cup cut string beans

Roux:
- 1 cup butter
- 1 cup flour

Make roux by melting one cup butter in saucepan. Stir in flour and heat until boiling. Reduce heat. Stir constantly until dark brown. Don't overbrown or overcook. This will not work in the microwave oven since the microwave will not allow the browning process to occur. Set aside.

Cook meat and onion in oil five minutes on high. Drain. Combine with remaining ingredients. Stir the roux into ingredients until completely blended. Cook on high five minutes. Stir. Cook on simmer for 25 to 30 minutes. Serve steaming with sourdough bread.

VENISON PEPPERS

Serves: 4

- 1 lb. ground venison
- 4 medium green peppers
- 1 onion, chopped
- 1 tsp. sage
- 1 clove garlic, minced
- 1 T. soy sauce
- 1½ cups cooked rice
- 1 cup tomato sauce

Cut the tops off peppers. Remove the seeds and rinse them thoroughly. Place peppers in a shallow microproof dish. Add enough water to cover bottom of dish. Cover and micro on high two minutes. Allow peppers to sit covered while you prepare filling.

Filling: in medium microproof dish, combine onion and crumbled ground meat. Micro on high four minutes or until meat is cooked, stirring once or twice to break up meat. Add sage, garlic, soy sauce, rice and tomato sauce. Fill peppers, packing well. Place stuffed peppers in casserole dish. Add 2 T. water to the bottom of the dish. Cover well. Micro on high eight to 10 minutes or until the peppers are tender. Allow to sit two to three minutes, covered, before serving to finish cooking.

EASY VENISON RAGOUT

Serves: 4

1 lb. venison stew meat, cut in 1-inch cubes
1 pkg. brown gravy mix
2 T. flour
    freshly ground pepper
1 clove garlic, minced
1 tsp. Worcestershire sauce
¼ cup Burgundy wine
2 carrots, sliced
2 potatoes, peeled and cubed
1 cup frozen peas, thawed and drained
1 cup beef broth

Lightly brown the venison in browning dish or skillet. Remove meat to 3-quart casserole. Add gravy mix and stir well. Add remaining ingredients. Stir well. Cook on 50 percent for 35 minutes or until meat and vegetables are tender. Stir occasionally during cooking time. Let stand three to four minutes before serving.

VENISON STEW

Serves: 4-6

> 2 lbs. venison stew meat, cut in small cubes
> flour
> bacon fat
> 3 carrots, sliced
> 3 small zucchini, chopped
> 2 potatoes, cut in chunks
> 4 fresh medium tomatoes, quartered

Marinade:

> 1-1½ cups Burgundy wine
> 1 cup beef bouillon
> 2 T. oil
> 12 peppercorns
> 2 garlic cloves, minced
> a few grindings of fresh pepper

Mix venison with marinade ingredients. Cover and refrigerate at least four hours. Drain the venison but reserve the marinade. Dust the venison with flour and brown in bacon fat in either skillet or microwave browning dish. Place the cubes in a 3-quart casserole dish. Add remaining ingredients and reserved marinade. Cover. Micro on high three to five minutes or until boiling. Reduce to 50 percent or simmer and cook for 30 minutes.

THREE BEAN ELK CHILI

Serves: 6-8

  1 lb. ground elk
  1 green pepper, diced
  1 onion, diced
  2 cloves garlic, minced
  1 28 oz. can whole tomatoes
  1 15 oz. can pinto beans
  1 15 oz. can kidney beans
  1 15 oz. can black-eyed peas
  1 tsp. salt
  1 tsp. pepper
  3 T. chili powder
  ¼ tsp. cayenne pepper
  1 tsp. cumin

Combine meat, pepper, onion and garlic in medium microproof saucepan. Micro on high four minutes. Stir to break up the meat. Micro on high two minutes more. Stir. In 4-quart casserole combine meat mixture and the remaining ingredients. Adjust seasonings to taste. Cover well. Micro on high five minutes or until boiling. Micro on simmer or 50 percent power for 25 to 30 minutes. Let sit four to five minutes to continue cooking before serving.

Note: Canned beans provide better results when cooked in a microwave than cooked dried beans.

ELK SIRLOIN STEAKS

Serves: 4

4 sirloin-cut elk steaks, about 8 oz. each
3 T. soy sauce
2 T. steak sauce
¼ onion, coarsely chopped
¼ tsp. ground pepper
2 stalks celery, sliced

In a small bowl, mix soy sauce, steak sauce, onions and pepper. In a 2-quart casserole, layer one steak with sauce, then continue layering steaks and sauce until steaks are stacked one on top of the other. Add celery around the steaks. Place temperature probe into the middle of the steaks. Cover with wax paper and micro on 80 percent until the temperature reaches 140 degrees, about 15 to 20 minutes. About halfway through, rearrange the steaks so they cook evenly. Cover with foil for five minutes before serving to continue cooking outside the oven.

Note: The meat will be a little pink when cooked in this manner. Cook to a higher temperature if you wish to have the meat well-done. My advice is to serve the meat a little pink inside so it doesn't toughen up.

ELK STEAK PIZZAIOLA

Serves: 2-4

- 1 **large elk steak, cut into serving pieces**
- 3 **T. olive oil**
- 1 **clove garlic, chopped**
- 2 **cups whole tomatoes, chopped**
- 1 **tsp. oregano**
- ½ **tsp. ground black pepper**

In a heavy stovetop skillet, heat olive oil and add garlic. Cook garlic until just barely brown. Lightly brown the steaks for a minute or two in the hot oil. Remove the steaks from the oil and place in the bottom of an 8-inch glass baking dish. Pour the tomatoes, oregano and black pepper into the skillet. Bring to a boil and then simmer for two to three minutes. Pour the tomatoes and spices over the elk steaks in the baking dish. Cover loosely. Micro on 70 percent for five to seven minutes or until cooked to your tastes. Allow to sit for a few minutes before serving.

GERMAN STYLE CARIBOU POT ROAST

Serves: 6

4 lb. caribou roast	2 cloves garlic
2 T. oil	salt and pepper
½ tsp. pepper	¼ tsp. ginger
1 cup water	¼ cup catsup
¼ cup flour	2 T. vinegar

In a large skillet, heat the oil and brown the outside of the roast. Season with pepper. Remove to large casserole. Stir water into the skillet and scrape to remove the sediment. Pour water into casserole. Insert temperature probe into the center of the meat and micro on 70 percent or roast until the temperature reaches 130 degrees. Remove roast to platter and cover with foil, shiny side down to finish cooking. Blend flour with the juices in the casserole. Micro on 50 percent for five minutes. Stir in two cloves garlic, salt, pepper, ginger, catsup and vinegar. Micro on 50 percent for four to five minutes. Pour gravy over the roast before serving.

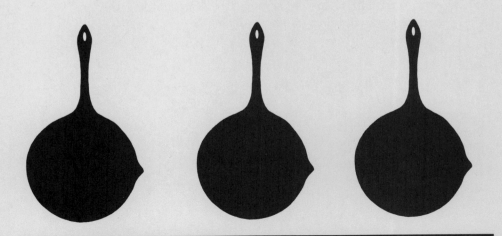

LEG OF WILD BOAR

Serves: 6

1 **wild boar leg**
2 **cloves garlic, slivered**
1 **T. fennel seeds**
3 **T. oil**
2 **tsp. poultry seasoning**
   freshly ground pepper
   flour (optional)

Cut the excess fat off the leg. Cut thin slits in the roast all over. Insert a sliver of garlic and a few fennel seeds in each slit. Heat the oil in a heavy skillet. Brown the outside of the roast on all sides. Place the roast in a baking dish. Sprinkle the remaining fennel seeds over the outside of the roast. Dust with poultry seasoning. Grind black pepper liberally over the roast. Insert temperature probe or microproof thermometer in the thickest part of the roast, making sure not to touch the bone. Cover loosely with plastic wrap. Micro at 60 percent or bake until the temperature reaches 165 degrees. Turn the roast over halfway through the cooking time to ensure even cooking. (Wild boar should be cooked thoroughly.) Remove from oven and cover with foil, shiny side down, to finish cooking. Serve with the pan drippings. Thicken the drippings with flour, if you wish.

STEWED UP RACCOON

Serves: 5-6

1 raccoon, cut
  into serving pieces
2-3 T. salt
½ cup white vinegar

1 onion, quartered
2 carrots, cut up
2 cups beef broth
12 peppercorns

In large bowl, mix raccoon, water to cover, salt and vinegar. Marinate overnight. Place raccoon pieces in a 2-quart casserole dish. Place the separated onion pieces and carrots on top of the meat. Pour the beef broth over the meat and vegetables. Sprinkle the peppercorns over the mixture. Cover tightly and micro on 50 percent or simmer for 25 minutes. Allow to sit for five minutes before serving.

BAKED WILD BOAR CHOPS

Serves: 2-4

4 boar chops
3-4 T. oil
½ cup maple syrup
4 T. catsup

1 tsp. dried mustard
1 tsp. cider vinegar
cornstarch (optional)

Cut the excess fat off the chops. Heat the oil in a heavy skillet and brown the chops quickly. Place the chops in a glass baking dish. Mix the maple syrup, catsup, mustard and vinegar in a small bowl. Stir until the mustard is dissolved. Pour the sauce over the chops. Micro on 70 percent or roast for eight to ten minutes until the juices run clear. (Wild boar should be cooked thoroughly.) Remove from oven and cover with foil for three to five minutes before serving. Thicken the sauce with cornstarch, if desired. Spoon the sauce over the chops.

SQUASH AND SQUIRRELS

Serves: 4

- 2 squirrels, cut in pieces
- 3 T. butter
- ½ medium onion, sliced
- 2 cups chicken bouillon
- 4 small crookneck squash (about 2½ cups), sliced

Roux:
- ½ cup butter
- ½ cup flour

Melt 3 T. butter in frying pan. Add onions and saute until transparent. Add squirrels, cook three to four minutes each side. Put squirrels and onions in 3-quart casserole. Add bouillon and squash. Cover. Micro on 70 percent for 10 minutes.

Meanwhile make roux. Melt butter in saucepan on stove. When butter is hot, add flour. Reduce heat and cook until caramel colored, stirring constantly. Squirrels may be done by this time. Let sit while making roux. Remove squirrels from bouillon. Stir in roux until well combined. Add more bouillon if too thick. Return squirrels to mixture. Micro on 70 percent or roast setting for 10 to 12 minutes until juices of squirrel run clear.

Note: the roux won't work in the microwave since there's no direct heat to brown the mixture.

BREADED BAKED SQUIRREL

Serves: 4

3 squirrels,
   cut into pieces
½ cup bread crumbs
2 T. cornmeal
¼ tsp. dry mustard
¼ tsp. chicken bouillon

1 T. parsley flakes
½ tsp. onion powder
   salt and pepper
   paprika
   Hot Mustard Sauce

Combine bread crumbs, cornmeal, dry mustard, parsley flakes, bouillon powder, onion powder, salt and pepper in a bag. Add squirrel pieces. Shake to coat squirrel. Place squirrel pieces in an 8- or 9-inch square baking dish. (It will take two layers.) Cover with plastic wrap. Micro on 70 percent power or roast setting for 20 minutes. Let sit covered for five minutes to finish cooking. Sprinkle pieces with paprika. Serve with Hot Mustard Sauce for individual dipping.

HOT MUSTARD SAUCE

Yield: ¾ cup

1 T. butter
1 T. flour
   salt and pepper

¾ cup milk
3 T. prepared mustard
1 T. horseradish

Micro butter on high one minute. Blend in flour, salt and pepper. Slowly stir in milk. Micro on 50 percent for two minutes. Stir in mustard and horseradish. Micro on 50 percent for one minute. Serve warm.

RABBIT CACCIATORE

Serves: 4

2 rabbits, quartered
  salt and pepper
¼ cup olive oil
½ medium onion, chopped
2 cloves garlic, minced
¼ cup dry white wine
2 T. white vinegar
¼ cup chicken bouillon
½ tsp. dried oregano
1 bay leaf
3 T. black olive slivers
1 T. capers

Rinse the rabbit with cold water and pat dry. Season the pieces with a little salt and a few grindings of fresh black pepper. Heat the olive oil in a heavy skillet and add the rabbit pieces. Brown on all sides. Move the rabbit to a plate. Pour the leftover oil in a 3-quart casserole. Add onion and garlic and micro on high four minutes. Add the wine and vinegar and micro on high five minutes. Pour in bouillon and micro on high one minute. Add the rabbit pieces, oregano and bay leaf. Cover and micro on high three to five minutes or until sauce is boiling. Stir. Reduce power to 50 percent or bake and micro for 15 to 18 minutes until rabbit is cooked through. Arrange the pieces on a platter and cover with foil, shiny side down. Stir black olives and capers into the sauce. Mix 2 T. with a little of the hot sauce and then pour back into the rest of the sauce. Micro on high for one minute to thicken. Pour the sauce over the rabbit.

RABBIT IN WHITE WINE

Serves: 2

- 1 **large rabbit, cut in serving pieces**
- 3 **T. butter**
- 1 **onion, sliced**
- 1 **carrot, sliced**
- 2 **stalks celery, diced**
  salt and pepper
- ¼ **tsp. thyme**
- ¼ **tsp. marjoram**
- 1 **cup chicken bouillon**
- 2 **T. vinegar**
- ½ **cup dry white wine**
- ¼ **cup sour cream**

In 2-quart casserole, micro butter one minute on high to melt. Add onion, carrot and celery. Stir well to coat. Micro on high for two minutes. In a separate bowl combine salt, pepper, thyme, marjoram, bouillon, vinegar and wine. Mix thoroughly. Place rabbit pieces on top of vegetable mixture. Pour wine/seasoning mixture over rabbit pieces and vegetables. Cover and micro on high five minutes. Micro on bake or 60 percent for seven minutes. Stir. Micro on bake five minutes more. Stir in sour cream. Micro on bake five minutes to complete. Serve over buttered noodles or on a platter surrounded by fresh green vegetables such as broccoli.

MEXICAN RABBIT

Serves: 2-3

  1 rabbit, cut into serving pieces
  4 T. butter
  1 clove garlic, minced
     salt
  1 cup chicken bouillon
  1 onion, chopped
  1 green pepper, chopped
  ½ cup black olives, sliced
  2 cups tomatoes, chopped
  3 T. flour
  1 cup canned corn

In a heavy skillet, melt the butter and add the rabbit and garlic. Brown on all sides. Pour the rabbit, butter and garlic mixture into a glass dish. Add salt and bouillon. Cover and micro on high for five minutes. Reduce power to 50 percent or simmer and micro for 15 to 17 minutes until the rabbit is cooked through. Remove the meat from the bones and discard the bones. Save one cup of the cooking broth. In 2-quart casserole mix the onion, pepper, olives and tomatoes. Cover and micro on high for five minutes, stirring once during the cooking time. With a whisk, stir in the flour. Pour in the cooking broth from the rabbit. Micro on 80 percent for three to four minutes or until the mixture is thickened. In an 8-inch square baking dish, spoon the corn in an even layer. Place a layer of the rabbit meat on top of the corn. Add the tomato mixture on top of the rabbit. Cover well and micro on 70 percent or roast for five to eight minutes until heated through.

CURRIED SAGE GROUSE SALAD

Serves: 6-8

    4 cups cooked sage grouse, cut in chunks
    3 cups cooked white rice
    ½ cup raw cauliflower, thinly sliced
    ½ cup creamy French salad dressing
    1 cup mayonnaise
    1½ tsp. curry powder
    1 tsp. salt
    ¼ tsp. pepper
    ½ cup milk
    ½ cup green peppers, diced
    1 cup celery, thinly sliced
    ½ cup red onions, chopped
       Romaine lettuce
    ¼ cup chutney
    ¼ cup hard boiled eggs, chopped
    ¼ cup peanuts
    ¼ cup pineapple chunks
    ¼ cup banana, diced
    ¼ cup coconut, shredded

Combine rice with cauliflower and French dressing and refrigerate at least two hours. Combine mayonnaise, curry powder, salt and pepper. Slowly stir in the milk. Add sage grouse and toss. Refrigerate two to three hours. Just before you're ready to serve, combine rice and sage grouse mixture, then add green pepper, celery and onion. Serve on top of a platter lined with Romaine lettuce leaves. Serve with the chutney, eggs, peanuts, pineapple chunks, diced banana and shredded coconut.

SAVORY DOVES

Serves: 4-5

10 doves	2 T. onion, minced
¼ cup flour	½ tsp. seasoned salt
3 T. oil	1 cup chicken broth
½ tsp. paprika	¼ cup red wine
1 T. fresh parsley, minced	

Dust the doves with flour. In a skillet heat oil and brown the doves. Mix remaining ingredients and pour into 3-quart casserole dish. Add the doves, stir well and cover. Micro on 80 percent for 13 to 15 minutes, stirring once or twice during cooking time. Remove the doves and thicken the sauce with a little flour if desired.

CREAMY MUSHROOM DOVES

Serves: 3-4

10 doves	4 green onions, sliced
8 T. butter	1½ cups heavy cream
flour	2 T. flour
3 cups mushrooms, sliced	buttered noodles

In skillet, melt 4 T. butter. Lightly dust doves with flour and brown in melted butter. In a 2-quart casserole melt 4 T. butter on high one minute. Add mushrooms and onions. Stir well, cover and micro on high four minutes. Pour in cream and stir well. Add doves and stir to coat. Cover, micro on 80 percent for 10 minutes. Stir. Remove from microwave. Remove ½ cup of the liquid. Stir in 2 T. flour. Return mixture to doves and stir well to combine. Micro on 80 percent for three minutes more. Stir well. Cover with foil and allow to sit for five minutes before serving over buttered noodles.

DOVES OLE!

Serves: 3-4

- 6 **doves**
- 4 **T. olive oil**
  salt and pepper
- ½ **onion, chopped finely**
- ½ **green pepper, sliced thinly**
- 1 **clove garlic, minced**
- 1 **cup carrots, chopped finely**
- 1 **cup celery, chopped**
- ¾ **cup tomato juice**
- 1 **bay leaf**
- ¼ **cup black olives, sliced**

In skillet brown the doves in olive oil. Arrange doves in 8-inch square baking dish. Sprinkle with salt and pepper. In a medium saucepan add a little fat from the skillet, onion, green pepper and garlic and micro on high for four minutes. Add the carrots, celery, tomato juice and bay leaf. Stir well and pour over doves. Cover tightly and micro on 80 percent for 13 minutes. Remove from microwave and add black olives. Cover with foil, shiny side down, for five minutes before serving.

ROAST PHEASANT

Serves: 2

1 pheasant
  salt and pepper
1 bay leaf

1 clove garlic
  a few celery leaves
2 T. butter, melted

Sauce:

½ cup consomme
2 T. flour
2 T. butter, melted
3 T. Madeira wine

Sprinkle the inside and the outside of the pheasant with the pepper. Add salt. Place the bay leaf, garlic and celery leaves on the inside of the pheasant. Tie the legs together with string. Insert temperature probe or microproof meat thermometer. Cover the bird loosely. Micro on 70 percent or roast until the temperature reaches 170 to 180 degrees and the juices from the bird run clear. Remove from the microwave and brush with butter. Brown under the broiler of your conventional oven.

Sauce: add the consomme to the drippings from the pan. Micro on high for two minutes. Blend the flour with the butter and stir into the gravy a little at a time. Micro on 90 percent or reheat for two to three minutes until thickened. Stir well then add the wine. Serve the pheasant with wine sauce.

CHEESY CHEDDAR PHEASANT

Serves: 2-3

- 1 **pheasant, quartered**
- ½ **medium onion, chopped**
- 1 **can cheddar cheese soup**
- ½ **cup buttermilk**
- 1 **T. Worcestershire sauce**
- ¾ **tsp. salt**
- ½ **medium onion, chopped**
- 1 **clove garlic, minced**
- 1 **cup mushrooms, sliced**
   buttered or spinach noodles

Mix soup, buttermilk, Worcestershire sauce, salt, onion, garlic and mushrooms. Stir well. Arrange pheasant pieces in casserole dish. Cover with sauce. Cover dish. Micro on high five minutes. Cook 15 to 20 minutes on bake or medium setting, until juices are no longer pink. Stir sauce and rearrange pheasant pieces once or twice during cooking. Be careful not to pierce the skin of the pheasant while turning the pieces or stirring. By not piercing the skin you won't lose any of the bird's juices. Serve pheasant and sauce over buttered or spinach noodles. Sprinkle with paprika.

QUAIL IN PARMESAN SAUCE

Serves: 4

8 quail	¾ cup light cream
salt and pepper	⅓ cup Parmesan cheese
5 T. butter	3 egg yolks, beaten
2 T. flour	½ cup fresh bread crumbs

Season the quail with salt and pepper. In skillet, melt half the butter and brown quail on both sides. In a microproof saucepan, micro remaining butter on high one minute. Add flour and stir with a whisk until blended. In a separate saucepan, micro cream on high three to five minutes or until boiling. Add all at once to flour/butter mixture, stirring until blended. Add 1 T. cheese to the mixture. When the cheese is melted, stir in the egg yolks. Sprinkle the bottom of a glass baking dish with ¼ cup cheese. Arrange the quail on the cheese and spoon the sauce over the top of the birds. Cover tightly. Micro on 60 percent or bake for 15 to 18 minutes.

QUAIL MARSALA

Serves: 4

8 quail	1 T. flour
3 T. oil	½ cup chicken broth
¼ cup butter	4 T. Marsala wine
¼ cup Canadian bacon	1 bay leaf
1 small onion, chopped	

Heat oil in skillet and brown the birds. Place the birds in a large baking dish. In a small saucepan, micro butter on high for one minute. Add the chopped Canadian bacon and onion. Micro on high for five minutes. Stir in flour, bouillon, Marsala and the bay leaf. Pour over the quail. Micro on 80 percent for 10 to 12 minutes. Place the quail on pieces of toasted French bread and cover with the Marsala mixture.

BRANDIED WOODCOCK

Serves: 2-3

- 4 woodcocks
- 4 T. butter
- ½ medium onion, finely chopped
- 2 T. brandy
- ¼ cup beef bouillon
  freshly ground pepper
- 2 cups baby carrots
- 2 T. flour
  fresh parsley, chopped

In a large skillet melt butter. Add onions and cook for two to three minutes. Add woodcocks and brown on all sides. Pour in brandy and flame with a match. Pour woodcock mixture into a 2-quart casserole. Stir in bouillon, pepper and baby carrots. Cover and micro on 80 percent for eight to ten minutes. Move the woodcocks and the carrots from the mixture to a warm platter and cover with foil. Add 2 T. flour to the liquid and stir well. Return the sauce to the microwave and cook for three minutes at 80 percent. Pour the sauce over the woodcocks (not over the carrots). Garnish the carrots with freshly chopped parsley.

CHUKAR TETRAZZINI

Serves: 6

1½ cups cooked chukar, cubed
 6 T. butter
 1 cup mushrooms
 ¼ cup flour
 ½ tsp. freshly ground pepper
 ¾ cup chicken bouillon
 1 cup heavy cream
 1 pkg. (7 oz.) spaghetti, cooked and drained
 2 stalks celery, sliced
 ½ cup grated Parmesan cheese

In a small saucepan, micro 2 T. butter one minute on high.
Add mushrooms and micro on high for four minutes. Set
aside. In a large saucepan, micro 4 T. butter on high for
one minute. Stir in flour, pepper, bouillon and cream.
Micro on 70 percent or roast for four to six minutes until
boiling. Allow to boil for one minute. Stir in spaghetti,
chukar, celery and mushrooms.

Pour into 2-quart casserole. Sprinkle with cheese. Cover
loosely. Micro on 80 percent or reheat for four to five
minutes until heated through. If you want the cheese topping browned, place it under the broiler in your oven for a
few minutes.

DR. TOM'S 40 GARLIC CHUKAR

   4 **chukars**
  ½ **onion, cut in half and separated into sections**
  1 **tsp. dried parsley**
  1 **tsp. thyme**
  4 **bay leaves, whole**
  1 **bay leaf, crushed**
  ⅔ **cup olive oil**
  1 **tsp. ground sage**
  1 **tsp. rosemary, crumbled**
  1 **tsp. dried thyme**
     salt and pepper
 40 **unpeeled garlic cloves (about 4 large heads garlic)**
  3 **T. water**

Separate the onion sections. Keep the four smallest ones. In each of the four sections sprinkle ¼ tsp. parsley, ¼ tsp. thyme and one whole bay leaf. Set aside. In a heavy skillet heat olive oil. Add crumbled bay leaf, sage, rosemary and dried thyme to oil. Add chukars and brown on all sides. Remove from oil and dust with salt and pepper.

Stuff an onion section into each body cavity. Tie legs together with string to hold onion in place. Put small pieces of foil around ends of legs to keep from overcooking. Make sure pieces of foil do not touch each other and are at least one inch from oven walls. Place birds in an 8-inch square glass dish. Put garlic cloves around birds and add water to bottom of dish. Cover tightly, micro on 60 percent or bake for 18-19 minutes. Remove from oven, cover with foil, shiny side down, for at least five minutes before serving.

Note: Small pieces of foil to protect tips of legs should only be used in new model microwave ovens. **Do not** *use foil in older microwaves. If in doubt,* **do not** *use foil.*

WILD RICE AND SAUSAGE STUFFED GOOSE

Serves: 4-6

 1 **goose, rinsed and patted dry**
 2 **T. butter, melted**
 2 **tsp. sage**

Stuffing:
 ½ **lb. pork or game sausage, cooked**
 3 **cups cooked wild rice**
 2 **T. butter, melted**
 3 **stalks celery, sliced**
 ½ **medium onion, chopped**

Mix all stuffing ingredients together in a large bowl. Stir well to combine. Loosely stuff goose. Truss the goose, if desired, and tie the legs together with string. Shield tips of legs with small pieces of foil to prevent overcooking. Make sure pieces of foil do not touch each other and are at least one inch from oven walls.

Mix together the melted butter and sage and brush over the outside of the goose. Insert the temperature probe in the thickest part of the goose between the leg and breast. Micro on 70 percent or roast until the temperature reaches 180 to 185 degrees. This normally takes about 30 to 40 minutes, depending on the size of the bird. Turn goose over halfway through cooking time to ensure complete cooking.

Note: Small pieces of foil to protect tips of legs should only be used in new model microwave ovens. **Do not** *use foil in older microwaves. If in doubt,* **do not** *use foil.*

APPLE ORCHARD GOOSE

Serves: 4-6

1 **goose, rinsed and dried**

Stuffing:
  3 **cups cooking apples, cored and sliced thinly**
  3 **T. lemon juice**
  1 **cup golden raisins**
  ½ **cup sugar**
  1 **tsp. ground cinnamon**
  ¼ **tsp. ground nutmeg**
2-3 **cardamom seeds, crushed**

Sauce:
  1 **cup apple jelly**
2-3 **T. cider vinegar, to taste**

Mix all stuffing ingredients together, stir well. Lightly
stuff the goose with the apple mixture. Tie the legs of the
goose together if desired. Placed small pieces of foil over
the tips of the legs to prevent overcooking. Make sure
pieces of foil do not touch each other and are at least one
inch from oven wall. Place bird in baking dish. Mix the
sauce ingredients together and spoon 2 to 3 T. of sauce
over the bird. Insert temperature probe into the thickest
part of bird. Cover loosely and micro on 70 percent or roast
until the temperature reaches 180 to 185 degrees. This
will usually take between 30 and 40 minutes, depending
on the size of the goose. Turn goose over halfway through.
Remove goose from oven, remove probe and cover tightly
with foil while you heat the sauce. Leave covered for at
least five minutes before serving. Heat the sauce on high
for three to four minutes or until heated thoroughly. Serve
the sauce with the goose.

*Note: See previous recipe regarding use of foil in
microwave.*

EASY DUCK SOUP

Serves: 4

**4-5 duck breasts, boned and chopped into 1-inch
       cubes
   4 T. butter
   1 onion, chopped
   3 cups beef bouillon
   2 bay leaves
   ½ tsp. garlic powder
       salt and freshly ground pepper
   1 cup soup mix or barley**

Melt butter in skillet. Add onions and cook for three to
four minutes or until onion is soft. Add duck breasts and
cook, stirring until duck breasts are browned on all sides.
Transfer duck meat and onions to a 2-quart casserole. Add
two cups of the bouillon and seasonings. Cover, micro on
high three minutes. Reduce heat to 50 percent or simmer
and cook for 20 minutes. Add soup mix or barley and more
beef bouillon. Cover loosely. Micro on high for three
minutes. Reduce heat to 50 percent or simmer and cook for
20 minutes. Allow to sit for a few minutes before serving.

DUCKS WITH BACON AND ONIONS

Serves: 3-4

7-8 breasts from large ducks
½ lb. bacon, cut in thirds
1 medium onion, cut in rings
   salt and freshly ground pepper
   flour

In a large casserole, combine bacon and onions. Dust with salt and pepper. Cover and micro on high for six minutes, stirring once or twice. Dust duck breasts lightly with flour. Add duck breasts to onion and bacon mixture. Micro on 60 percent for 18 to 19 minutes or until juices run clear. Stir once or twice while cooking. Remove from oven and cover with foil, shiny side down to finish cooking for at least five minutes.

CHERRY SAUCED DUCK BREASTS

Serves: 3-4

2½-3 lbs. large duck breasts (about 8)
   1 onion, sliced thinly
   2 oranges, separated into segments
   1 cup Tangy Cherry Sauce

In a 2-quart casserole, combine duck breasts with onions and oranges. Pour sauce over the duck breast mixture. Cover well and micro on 70 percent or roast 15 to 18 minutes. Let sit five minutes before serving to finish cooking. Pour leftover cherry sauce over duck breasts before serving. Pass the remaining sauce at the table. (The oranges and onions can be removed if so desired.)

TANGY CHERRY SAUCE

Yield: 1½ cups

   1 lb. bing cherries, chopped coarsely
   ¼ cup lemon juice
   1 cup water
   ½ cup sugar
   2 T. cornstarch

Combine lemon juice, water, sugar and cornstarch in large saucepan. Stir until sugar is dissolved. Add cherries. Micro on high 10 to 12 minutes until thickened. Stir once during cooking.

ALL PURPOSE GAME MARINADE

Yield: 2 cups

½ cup oil	½ tsp. salt
1½ cups white vinegar	6 T. Worcestershire sauce
¼ tsp. liquid smoke	1 tsp. peppercorns
1 bay leaf	

Combine all ingredients. Refrigerate well before using.

Note: Good for dry cuts of game such as flank steaks, small game with little fat or round steaks.

STUFFED MUSHROOMS

Serves: 24-30 appetizers

1 lb. large fresh mushrooms
¼ lb. game sausage
1 clove garlic, minced
¼ cup onion, minced
1 T. fresh parsley, minced
1 tsp. Kitchen Bouquet
¼ cup sour cream
2 T. Parmesan cheese

Remove stems from mushrooms. Set aside. Combine sausage, garlic, onion, parsley and Kitchen Bouquet and stir well. Micro on high for four to five minutes or until sausage is cooked (not overcooked, though). Stir in sour cream and cheese. Fill each mushroom with sausage mixture. Arrange 10 to 12 mushrooms on a plate. Micro on 70 percent power or roast for three to five minutes until heated through. Repeat with remaining mushrooms.

JOE GREEN'S CHUKAR BITS

Serves: 36 appetizers

12 slices bacon
8 oz. chukar meat, cut in small chunks
¼ tsp. garlic powder
¼ cup soy sauce

Cut bacon into thirds. Mix garlic powder in soy sauce. Dip chukar pieces in soy sauce and wrap in ⅓ slice bacon. Secure with wooden toothpicks. Place 12 at a time on a paper towel-lined plate. Cover with paper towels. Micro on high four to five minutes or until bacon is crisp.

ASPARAGUS VINAIGRETTE

Serves: 6-8

1 lb. asparagus
1 T. olive oil
1 T. white vinegar
2 T. lemon juice
1 tsp. Dijon mustard
¼ tsp. rosemary

Trim woody ends off asparagus stalks. Lay flat on microproof baking dish or plate. Add 2 to 3 T. water. Cover tightly with plastic wrap. Mix remaining ingredients in small saucepan. Place both asparagus and the vinaigrette in microwave. Micro on high for three to four minutes. Remove both from oven. Combine both in serving bowl, toss to cover asparagus completely with vinaigrette.

MEMBERS RECIPES

MARINATED VENISON STEAKS

Serves: 4
Prep Time: 30 minutes

4 venison steaks
Marinade:

1 cup red wine	**salt and pepper**
½ cup brown sugar	**¼ cup onion, minced**
¼ cup catsup	**⅓ cup fresh mushrooms,**
⅛ cup molasses	**minced**
1 1 cestershire	

In ble   er, mix all marinade ingredients except onion and
mush oms. After ingredients are well mixed, stir in onion
and mushrooms. Place meat in container, cover well with
marinade. Cover and put in refrigerator overnight, turning meat occasionally. Drain excess marinade from steaks
and either broil or grill, brushing with leftover marinade
while cooking.

Valarie Waldron
Minneapolis, Minnesota

STUFFED VENISON STEAK

Serves: 6
Prep Time: 1½ hours

  2 **lbs. venison steak, cut ¾-inch thick**
1½ **cups milk**
  6 **slices bacon**
⅓ **cup chopped green onion**
    salt and pepper
½ **cup cold water**
¼ **cup flour**

Cut venison steak into six serving size pieces. Place in shallow pan, pour milk over meat. Cover and refrigerate overnight, turning meat several times. Drain meat, pat dry with paper towels. Cook bacon until crisp. Drain, reserving 2 T. drippings. Crumble bacon and set aside.

With sharp knife, carefully cut a pocket in one side of each piece of meat. Mix bacon and green onion. Stuff onion mixture into pockets of meat. In 10-inch skillet, brown steaks in reserved bacon drippings. Season with salt and pepper. Add ½ cup water. Cover and simmer over low heat until tender, 45 to 60 minutes. Remove meat to platter.

For gravy, measure pan juices; add enough water to make 1½ cups. Blend ½ cup cold water slowly into flour. Stir into pan juice mixture. Cook, stirring constantly until mixture bubbles and thickens. Season to taste with salt and pepper, pour over meat.

Gayle Heilman
Millbury, Ohio

VENISON STEAK

Serves: 5
Prep Time: 15 minutes

2-3 lbs. tenderized and deboned steak or loin
** 1 cup flour**
** ½ tsp. salt**
** ½ tsp. pepper**
**   lard or cooking oil**

Mix flour, salt and pepper on paper plate. Coat steaks well
in this mixture. Fry in ½ inch oil or lard on high heat. The
secret is to fry the steak fast and in hot oil. Fry until
brown and enjoy.

Ken Vargason
Blairstown, Iowa

BREADED VENISON CHOPS
OR STEAK

Serves: 6
Prep Time: 50 minutes

** 1 egg**
** 2 T. water**
** 1 10½ oz. can cream of mushroom soup**
** 1 cup bread crumbs**
** 6 chops or equal amount of steak**

Beat egg together with water. Dip chops in egg mixture,
then coat with bread crumbs. Brown 10 to 15 minutes on
each side. Add mushroom soup thinned with ½ soup can of
water. Simmer for 30 minutes or until done.

Ronald Orr
Ogallala, Nebraska

VENISON IN BARBEQUE SAUCE

Serves: 4
Prep Time: 2 hours

Cut 2 lbs. venison into 1½- to 2-inch cubes and brown in bacon grease. Make barbeque sauce as follows:

½ cup catsup	1 tsp. salt
½ cup white vinegar	½ tsp. pepper
2 T. brown sugar	2 garlic cloves, pressed
2 T. Worcestershire sauce	1 T. lemon juice
½ tsp. or less Tabasco sauce	
2 small onions	

Slice onions into rings, cut in half and cook in bacon grease before adding to remainder of sauce ingredients. Bring sauce to a boil and simmer for 20 minutes. Stir in venison cubes, cover and cook at low heat about one hour or until tender. Sauce will thicken so add water while cooking, if needed. Makes good hors d'oeuvres served in hot chafing dish. Mixture or sauce alone can be served over rice or egg noodles. Sauce can be made in larger quantities, but reduce Tabasco to taste.

Ed Ballowe
Chatham, New Jersey

MARINATED VENISON STEAK

Serves: 4-6
Prep Time: overnight

3-4 **lbs. venison steak**
  1 **medium onion, minced**
  1 **T. vinegar**
    flour

1 **tsp. nutmeg**
1 **tsp. allspice**
 salt and pepper

Combine onion, vinegar, nutmeg and allspice with enough water to cover meat (in a glass dish) and allow to marinate overnight in refrigerator, covered. Stir once or twice.

When ready to cook, remove steaks from marinade, salt and pepper them and flour on both sides. Fry slowly in butter.

Patty Myers
Royersford, Pennsylvania

VENISON BARBEQUE

Serves: 4-5 sandwiches
Prep Time: 1 hour

1 lb. ground venison	1 T. catsup
1 cup water	celery seed
½ cup celery	4 oz. chili sauce
1 T. mustard	

Cook venison, water and celery together until celery is tender. Add mustard, catsup, celery seed (to taste) and chili sauce. Simmer, without lid for ½ hour. Serve on hamburger buns.

W. Paul Brandt
Mount Joy, Pennsylvania

VENISON CHILI

Serves: 2-4
Prep Time: 50 minutes

1 lb. ground venison with beef
1 chili stick
2 cans kidney beans
1 or 2 quarts tomato juice
1 T. chili powder

Brown venison and ground beef until it changes color and is done. Mix all other ingredients together and cook over low heat to boiling, then simmer for about ½ hour. Turn off stove and let chili sit until ready to serve.

Lorene Heugel
Leavenworth, Kansas

BARBEQUED VENISON RIB BAKE

Serves: 4
Prep Time: 1½ hours

2-3 lbs. venison ribs
2 T. oil
¼ tsp. salt
⅛ tsp. pepper
¼ cup flour
Barbeque sauce:
¼ cup chopped onion
4 T. brown sugar
⅛ tsp. pepper
½ cup catsup
3 T. vinegar
1 tsp. Worcestershire
½ cup apricot jam

Mix ingredients for barbeque sauce in order given. Cook barbeque sauce for five minutes over low heat until thick.

Wash ribs and drain on paper. Heat oil and season ribs with salt and pepper. Roll in flour. Fry until brown. Put into a baking dish and cover with barbeque sauce. Baste ribs with sauce as they bake at 350 degrees for 1½ hours or until done.

Paul W. Hills, Sr.
Kettle Falls, Washington

VENISON CHOPS

Serves: 4-6
Prep Time: 1½ hours

4-6 venison chops   brown mushroom soup
flour   salt and pepper
shortening

Dip chops in flour, brown quickly on both sides. Drain shortening off, mix brown mushroom soup with one can water, pour over chops. Simmer for one hour. Serve with mashed potatoes, green salad.

Dave Keith
Phoenix, Arizona

ITALIAN VENISON

Serves: 4
Prep Time: 8-10 hours

2-3 lb. deer roast   3 beef bouillon cubes
1 tsp. oregano   3 cups water
1 T. marjoram   1 T. Worcestershire
1 T. thyme   dash Tabasco
1 T. garlic powder   salt and pepper

Mix all ingredients and put in crock pot. Cook 8 to 10 hours or until meat falls apart. Cook onions, hot peppers, green and red mild peppers in water to serve over meat. Serve with baked potatoes and salad.

Gloria Jones
Charleston, Illinois

BILLY'S GREEN CHILI VENISON BURROS

Serves: 4
Prep Time: 2½ hours

    3-4 lbs. diced venison
      3 T. butter
1 or 2 diced onions
      1 7 oz. can whole green chilies
      1 7 oz. can diced green chilies
      1 12 oz. jar green chili salsa
      1 8 oz. can tomato sauce
      1 14½ oz. can stewed tomatoes
    ¾ tsp. salt
    ½ tsp. pepper
    ½ tsp. garlic salt

Brown venison in butter. Add diced onions, salt, pepper and garlic salt. Simmer for 10 minutes. Add the remaining ingredients and cook for 1½ to 2 hours. Serve rolled in flour tortillas.

Note: Better if made in cast iron Dutch oven.

William Boyda
Apache Junction, Arizona

VENISON ROAST

Serves: 7-9
Prep Time: 2 hours

Marinate a 5-6 lb. roast overnight in:
½ cup dry red wine
¼ cup olive oil
1 tsp. salt
1 T. crushed rosemary
½ tsp. black pepper
¼ tsp. powdered cloves
1 cup clove garlic

Place venison is roasting pan. Make a few slits in meat with sharp knife, spoon mixture over all. Cover meat with ½ lb. sliced bacon. In bottom of roasting pan put:

1 cup diced celery
1 cup diced carrots
1 cup diced onion
1 10½ oz. can beef consomme
    remaining marinade

Roast at 400 degrees for 15 minutes. Reduce heat to 350 degrees and roast about 1½ hours longer. Baste with pan drippings every 20 minutes. Remove roast to a platter. Strain pan drippings and thicken with flour to make gravy. Garnish meat with drained, chopped vegetables.

Edward Almeida
Petaluma, California

WALTER'S DEER

Serves: varies
Prep Time: 3-4 hours

1 **venison hindquarter, boned**
4 **strips bacon**
1 **large onion, sliced**
1 **large can mushrooms**
4 **carrots, diced**
4 **potatoes, diced**
2 **cloves garlic**
2 **bottles Italian dressing**
1 **pint dry white wine**
1 **tsp. red pepper**

Place bacon strips in open hindquarter. Sprinkle in red pepper and lightly salt. Add garlic, roll and tie. Place rolled hindquarter in deep pan. Add Italian dressing and wine. Place onion on top of meat, pour on mushrooms, carrots and potatoes. Place on covered charcoal grill with fire in one end and meat on the other for four hours. (Can be done in oven at 325 to 350 degrees for about 2½ hours or until done.) Baste occasionally.

When cooked, slice thin and serve either as entree or as sandwiches.

Walter L. Allen
Montgomery, Alabama

VENISON CARLOS

Serves: varies
Prep Time: 5 days

vension backstrap
buttermilk

Slice strips of backstrap about the thickness of thick sliced bacon. Cross hatch each strip. Place a layer of strips in a flat baking pan. Cover with buttermilk and continue to layer until all meat is in the pan. Place in refrigerator for five days.

Remove and place strips on charcoal grill for two to three minutes. Use as an appetizer.

Walter L. Allen
Montgomery, Alabama

VENISON MEATLOAF

Serves: 4
Prep Time: 1 hours 25 minutes

2½ lbs. ground venison with beef suet
 ¼ cup canned milk
  1 clove garlic, minced
  1 large onion, grated
  1 tsp. Worcestershire sauce
     salt and pepper

Place the ingredients in a large mixing bowl and mix thoroughly, then transfer to a well-oiled baking dish and let sit in a cool place for about 30 minutes so that the meat will absorb the seasoning. Bake in a preheated oven at 350 degrees for one hour. If you wish, lay one or two slices of bacon over the loaf before putting in oven.

Lorene Heugel
Leavenworth, Kansas

VENISON SCALLOPINI

Serves: 8
Prep Time: 2 hours

3 lbs. tender venison
butter and olive oil
1 bunch green onions
1 clove garlic
1 bunch parsley
2 sprigs fresh rosemary
1 pinch marjoram
2 small cans tomato sauce
1 large can sliced mushrooms
1 pint dry sauterne or sherry

About 45 minutes before preparing venison, start sauce. Heat small skillet, add half butter and half olive oil. After chopping very fine or using blender, add the following mixture and cook on medium heat for about 20 minutes: green onions (tops and all), garlic, parsley (not stems), rosemary (not stems) and marjoram. After 20 minutes add tomato sauce and mushrooms (save juice for later). Stir well and cook for an additional 10 minutes and then let simmer on low heat while cooking venison.

Cut venison into 3-inch squares and trim off all fat. Pound well and shake in seasoned flour (salt and pepper). This can be done while cooking sauce. Brown in hot skillet in half butter and half olive oil, about a minute on both sides. Add sauce and mix thoroughly. Let simmer for an additional 15 minutes. During last four minutes, add one full cup of sauterne or sherry. During last two minutes, add juice of mushrooms. Serve hot. Great when served with rice or polenta, also buttered noodles.

Harold Doughty
Napa, California

VENISON MEATLOAF

Serves: 8
Prep Time: 1 hour

- 1 lb. ground venison
- 1 lb. pork sausage
- ¾ cup crushed crackers
- ½ cup minced onion
- 2½ oz. sliced mushrooms
- 1 T. mustard
- 1 egg, slightly beaten
- ⅓ cup catsup
- ½ tsp. garlic salt
- ¼ tsp. pepper
- 1 T. Worcestershire sauce
- 1 T. A-1 Steak Sauce
- ½ tsp. curry powder
- ⅓ cup grated cheddar cheese

Combine all ingredients and shape into loaf in 13 x 9 x 2 baking dish. Bake in preheated oven at 350 degrees for about one hour. Let stand five minutes before slicing.

Donald R. Wyatt
Weyers Cave, Virginia

BOWHUNTER VENISON PIE

Serves: 6
Prep Time: 1½ hours

    1 **package (10 oz.) pastry mix**
    ½ **cup grated sharp cheddar cheese**
    ½ **tsp. paprika**
       dash of cayenne
   1½ **lbs. ground venison**
    1 **small onion, minced**
   1½ **cups dry bread cubes**
    1 **10 oz. can beef bouillon or consomme**
    ½ **tsp. salt**
    ¼ **tsp. thyme and marjoram**
    2 **T. Worcestershire sauce**

Prepare pastry mix as directed on the package, adding
cheese, paprika and cayenne before adding the liquid. Roll
half a pastry on lightly floured board, fit into 9-inch pie
pan. Cook beef and onion in skillet until meat loses its red
color, breaking up meat with fork. Drain excess grease.
Add Worcestershire sauce, thyme and marjoram, mix well.
Mix bread cubes and bouillon and let stand for a few
minutes. Add to beef, onion mixture, stirring until well
mixed, Pour into pastry-lined pan. Roll remaining pastry
and put over top crimping edges. Bake at 375 degrees for
about 45 minutes. Serve warm or cold.

*Note: You can use muffin pan for individual pies to take
hunting.*

Ed Botwright
Hyattsville, Missouri

VENISON POT STEW

Serves: 4
Prep Time: 2½ hours

3½ lbs. cubed venison
¼ cup flour
¼ cup shortening
1½ cups hot water
1 cup red wine
1 large onion, sliced
4 medium carrots
4 medium potatoes
thyme
marjoram
basil
fresh or dried parsley

Flour the meat. Preheat a heavy stew pot then add fat, fry
the meat and onion until light brown. Add water, wine,
herbs, salt and pepper. Cover, simmer for two hours. Add
carrots and potatoes. Cook until vegetables are done.
Serve with rice or noodles.

Bob Dubuque
Walpole, Massachusetts

INDIAN VENISON JERKY

Serves: varies
Prep Time: 3 days

> **venison**
> **salt**
> **pepper**

Cut five pounds of venison into ¼-inch strips. Salt and pepper each piece. Put in bowl with holes in bottom to drain. Let sit five hours in bowl, draining. Hang in cool place for three days and it's ready to eat.

Lewis Lytle
Las Vegas, Nevada

BAKED DEER JERKY

Serves: varies
Prep Time: 3-5 hours

3 lbs. venison	2 tsp. Accent
2 tsp. onion powder	½ cup soy sauce
2 tsp. seasoned salt	⅔ tsp. black pepper
½ cup Worcestershire sauce	⅔ tsp. garlic powder

Cut meat into ⅜-inch slices. Combine remaining ingredients and add meat. Marinate 12 to 24 hours. Place meat slices on oven racks, with foil underneath to catch drippings. Bake at 150 degrees for three to five hours or until dried.

Kenneth W. Crummett
Moyers, West Virginia

GROUND DEER JERKY

Serves: 12
Prep Time: 4-8 hours

2 lbs. lean ground venison
½ cup soy sauce
2 T. Worcestershire sauce
½ tsp. garlic powder
½ tsp. pepper
½ tsp. onion powder
1 tsp. Tabasco sauce
2 T. taco sauce
2 tsp. liquid smoke

Place ground meat in large bowl. Mix all ingredients together and pour over ground meat. Mix well, then place in refrigerator for 12 hours.

Roll out into thin strips or patties and place on cookie sheet. Bake at 150 degrees for four to eight hours. Drying time will depend on thickness of strips or patties. When dry store in container in refrigerator or freezer.

Ronald Orr
Ogallala, Nebraska

VENISON JERKY

Serves: 6
Prep Time: 13 hours

1½ lbs. flank steak
** 1 T. liquid smoke**
1⅓ T. garlic powder
1⅓ T. pepper
** 1 T. monosodium glutamate**
** 1 T. onion powder**
** ¼ cup soy sauce**
** ¼ cup Worcestershire sauce**
**   barbeque salt (if desired)**

Trim all possible fat off the meat, then slice ⅛-inch thick. Marinate overnight in a glass dish in the refrigerator. Turn occasionally to coat thoroughly. In the morning, drain well on paper, patting meat dry. Lay strips on a single layer on an oven rack being careful that they do not overlap. Place a cookie sheet or foil underneath to catch the drips. Roast at 120 degrees for 8 to 12 hours with oven door slightly ajar. Taste occasionally until it is as chewy as desired. Store in airtight containers.

Frank Kytchak
Greenville, Pennsylvania

VENISON JERKY

Serves: varies
Prep Time: 8-12 hours

- 2 **lbs. venison steak**
- ½ **cup soy sauce**
- 2 **T. lemon juice**
- 1 **tsp. ginger**
- ¼ **tsp. Tabasco sauce**
- 1 **tsp. liquid smoke**
- ½ **tsp. garlic salt**
- ¼ **tsp. pepper**

Mix together the soy sauce, lemon juice, ginger, Tabasco sauce, pepper, garlic salt and liquid smoke. Cut meat (with the grain) into one-inch strips. Put meat into bowl, pour mixture over meat and cover bowl. Let stand for six hours, then lay strips of meat on middle rack of oven (put foil below to catch drips) and bake at 150 to 200 degrees for 8 to 12 hours, leaving oven door open a crack.

Mike Johnson
Salem, Oregon

VENISON SWEDISH MEATBALLS

Serves: 6
Prep Time: 1 hour

1½ lbs. ground venison or half venison, half beef
1½ cups soft bread crumbs
1 cup light cream or milk
½ cup chopped onion
1 egg
¼ cup parsley flakes
1½ tsp. salt
2 T. flour
1 can beef consomme
¼ cup cold water
½ tsp. instant coffee
butter or margarine
dash pepper
dash nutmeg
¼ tsp. ginger

Soak bread in cream about five minutes. Cook onion in 1 T. butter or margarine until tender, but not brown. Combine meat, crumb mix, egg, onion, parsley and seasonings. Form into 1½-inch balls. Brown in skillet with 2 T. butter or margarine, shaking skillet to keep balls round. Remove meatballs. Mix flour and water and stir into drippings in skillet. Add broth and coffee. Replace meatballs, heat and serve.

Jim Peterson
Marshfield, Wisconsin

EASTER DAY VENISON

Serves: 5
Prep Time: 1 hour

3 lb. venison roast
5 big potatoes, peeled and chunked
5 carrots, peeled and sliced
3 medium onions, quartered
bacon
soy sauce
Worcestershire sauce
1 can Campbell's Vegetarian Vegetable
Alphabet soup
water

Heat covered electric fying pan to 350 degrees. Wrap entire roast in bacon strips and pin in place with toothpicks. Place in frying pan with ⅓ cup soy sauce and ⅔ cup water. Cover and allow to cook for 20 minutes. Add a 2 to 1 water/soy sauce mixture as needed to keep liquid in bottom of pan.

After 20 minutes add potatoes, carrots, onions and a dash of Worcestershire sauce. Cook for another 40 minutes, turning roast occasionally, stirring vegetables and basting as needed with water/soy sauce. In the last 10 minutes of cooking add the soup and one can of water.

To serve, remove bacon strips and slice roast ¼- to ½-inch thick. Pepper to taste and serve with fruit salad for a complete meal.

Bill Miller
Eau Claire, Wisconsin

ENCORE CHILI

Serves: 6 (12 servings)
Prep Time: 1½ hours

3 lbs. ground elk	1 T. soy sauce
2 medium onions	½ cup catsup
1 green pepper	2 packages chili mix
2 quarts tomatoes	1 tsp. dry mustard
1 can chili beans	1 T. chili powder
1 can kidney beans	½ tsp. salt
1 cup red wine	1 tsp. pepper
1 T. Worcestershire	

Brown meat, onions and green pepper. Combine all other ingredients in a large pan. Add meat, simmer for at least one hour.

Lynn Kinion
Delmar, Iowa

UPPER MICHIGAN ELK CHILI

Serves: 4-6
Prep Time: 1 hour

2 lbs. ground elk
1 large onion, diced
1 green pepper, diced
1 28 oz. can whole tomatoes
1 6 oz. can tomato paste
1 cup water
1 can kidney beans
½ tsp. garlic powder
2 tsp. salt
2 tsp. Italian seasoning
2 tsp. chili powder
2 tsp. black pepper or
1 tsp. crushed red pepper
elbow macaroni

Brown meat in a large pan that is about 4 inches deep.
Add onion and green pepper, tomatoes, tomato paste,
beans, garlic powder, salt, Italian seasoning, chili powder,
either the red or black pepper and about three fist fulls of
elbow macaroni.

Simmer at a low temperature and cover. It takes about one
hour from the time you start. You can tell when it's done
by tasting the noodles. . .when they are soft, it's done. Stir
every now and then so it doesn't stick to the bottom of pan.

John Zanon
Norway, Michigan

MOOSE ENCHILADAS

Serves: 6
Prep Time: 1 hour

> 1 **lb. ground moose (other game will work also)**
> 1 **clove garlic**
>   **small amount of chopped onion**
> 2 **cans enchilada sauce**
> 2 **cans water**
>   **salt and pepper**
>   **flour tortillas**
>   **grated cheddar cheese**
>   **Parmesan cheese**

Brown meat, clove and onion in a little bit of oil. Drain and set aside. Take enchilada sauce and water and simmer in frying pan until thickened. Salt and pepper meat and sauce to taste.

Mix together:
> 1 **bunch chopped green onions**
> 1 **chopped green pepper**
> 2 **large chopped tomatoes**
> 1 **small can chopped olives**

Dip flour tortillas quickly into sauce; lay on flat board and fill with meat, chopped vegetables, grated cheese and Parmesan cheese. Roll and place in buttered baking dish. Pour remaining sauce over and top with leftover vegetables and cheese. Cover and bake at 350 degrees for ½ hour.

Gerald Asher
Redding, California

ANTELOPE STEW

Serves: 4
Prep Time: 1½ to 2 hours

- **2 lbs. antelope meat, cubed**
- **2 T. bacon fat**
- **flour, salt and pepper**
- **1 can solid packed tomatoes**
- **¼ tsp. cumin seed**
- **¼ tsp. dried basil leaf**
- **½ tsp. celery seed**
- **5 carrots**
- **5 medium potatoes**
- **1 T. Worcestershire**
- **1 small can mushrooms**
- **1 onion, chopped**

Salt, pepper and flour meat and brown in bacon fat. Add onion, mushrooms and Worcestershire, stir until onion is light brown. Add enough water to cover meat. Add tomatoes and simmer for one hour. Add basil leaves, celery seed and cumin seed. Simmer for 30 minutes, then add potatoes and carrots. Cook until meat is tender.

Note: If mushroom sauce is used in place of mushrooms, add at the time that potatoes and carrots are added.

James Bresee
Pampa, Texas

COOKED WOODCHUCK

Serves: 4
Prep Time: 1 hour

1 chuck, cut up	garlic powder
1 cup corn meal	3 onions
1 cup flour	1 stalk celery
1 egg	½ stick butter
1 cup water	cooking oil
parsley	salt and pepper

Boil chuck with one onion and celery until tender. Cool meat and roll in flour until completely covered. Beat egg and one cup water together. Add seasonings to corn meal. Dip meat in egg/water mixture and then into corn meal until meat is completely coated. Cut remaining two onions into thin slices. Melt butter in skillet and add onions, fry until tender. Move onion to side but not out of skillet. Add enough cooking oil to bring level of oil to ¾ inch. Heat oil and add coated chuck. When coating is crisp on bottom side, turn chuck over and cut heat back to low or medium. Cover chuck with onions, cover pan and simmer for 15 minutes. Remove chuck and onions, salt and pepper to taste.

Paul Hatas
Walbridge, Ohio

STEVE'S BARBEQUE TURTLE

Serves: 4
Prep Time: 3½ hours

2 **snapping turtles, cleaned and boned**	1 **clove garlic**
2 **T. hot sauce**	1 **medium onion**
1 **T. black pepper**	1 **16 oz. bottle of Coke**
8 **oz. catsup**	1 **T. ReaLemon**
brown sugar	1 **hot pepper (optional)**

Boil turtle for 2½ hours or until tender. Drain off water.
Mix all ingredients together (add brown sugar to taste).
Heat until sugar dissolves. Place turtle in baking dish and
pour sauce over. Bake for one hour at 200 degrees, basting
every 20 minutes.

Steve Tabor
Jeffrey, West Virginia

BOAR ADOBO

Serves: 5-6
Prep Time: 1½ hours

2-3	lbs. boar meat, cut into 1½-inch chunks
1½	tsp. salt
15-20	peppercorns, whole
2-3	bay leaves
5	cloves garlic, finely chopped
2-inch	piece of ginger root, finely chopped or grated
¼ to ⅓	cup desired wine
⅓	cup vinegar
3-4	T. soy sauce
⅓	cup water

Brown meat in small amount of vegetable oil at fairly high heat. Set aside. Drain off excess oil. Saute garlic and ginger root in the remaining oil. Mix together the remaining ingredients. Add meat and other ingredients to garlic and ginger in pot. Simmer slowly, stirring occasionally, until desired doneness.

Note: Recipe may be used for store bought pork with the amounts of seasonings adjusted as desired.

Ray A. Fabrao
Lanai City, Hawaii

BAKED COTTONTAIL

Serves: 3
Prep Time: 1 hour

1 rabbit, cut into serving pieces
4 T. butter or margarine
½ cup flour
3-4 potatoes, sliced
3-4 carrots, sliced
1 can cream of mushroom soup
1 cup water
1 tsp. meat tenderizer

Rub pieces of rabbit with meat tenderizer, flour and brown in butter or margarine in skillet. Place rabbit in baking dish and add potatoes, carrots and water. Spread undiluted mushroom soup over top of rabbit and vegetables. Bake in oven at 350 degrees for 45 minutes or until tender.

Byron Banta
Muncie, Indiana

BUNNY SAUSAGE

Serves: 8
Prep Time: 1 hour

6	deboned rabbits	¾	cup milk
2	small onions, minced	¼	tsp. paprika
2	T. salt	1	bay leaf
2	tsp. pepper	½	tsp. ground sage
½	cup bread crumbs	2	eggs, well beaten

Grind rabbit meat. Add all ingredients and mix well. Make into patties. Fry until well done or freeze until the mood strikes.

Lawrence J. Kuster
Hamlin, New York

SWEET AND SOUR HASENPFEFFER

Serves: 6
Prep Time: 3 hours

1 rabbit	2 T. fat
1 quart vinegar	2 T. flour
2 T. salt	1 cup cold water
1 T. pickling spice	1 tsp. cinnamon
1 T. peppercorns	½ tsp. allspice
2 large onions, sliced	

Cut rabbit into serving portions, place in a crock and cover with vinegar combined with salt, spices, peppercorns and one onion. Let stand in a cool place for 24 hours. Drain, cover with boiling water and simmer until tender, about 1½ hours. Remove meat and strain broth. Melt fat in a frying pan, blend in flour and add water, stirring constantly. Cook until thickened. Add rabbit, strained broth, cinnamon, allspice and remaining onion and simmer for one hour.

Boyd Miller
Fremont, Louisiana

COUNTRY CAPTAIN

Serves: 4-6
Prep Time: 1 hour 15 minutes

3½ lbs. squirrel or rabbit, cut up
 ⅓ cup flour
1¾ tsp. monosodium glutamate
 ½ tsp. salt
 ¼ tsp. pepper
 ½ cup oil
1½ cups green pepper, finely chopped
 1 cup onion, finely chopped
 1 clove garlic, minced
 2 tsp. curry powder
 ½ tsp. thyme
 1 1-lb. can tomatoes
 1 tsp. snipped parsley
 1 cup almonds, blanched and split in half
 1 T. butter
 ½ cup currants
 8 cups hot cooked rice

Combine flour with next three ingredients. Coat meat pieces with flour mixture. Brown on all sides in hot oil in heavy skillet. Remove meat from skillet to a 3-quart baking dish. Add green pepper, onion and garlic to drippings. Cook until softened but not brown. Blend in salt, pepper, curry powder and thyme. Add tomatoes and parsley. Pour mixture over meat. Cover and bake at 350 degrees for about 45 minutes or until fork tender. Brown almonds lightly in butter. To serve, arrange in center of large heated platter. Pile rice around.Add currants to hot sauce to plump them. Pour over meat. Sprinkle almonds over sauce.

Donald Kerr
Chebanse, Illinois

RITA'S SQUIRREL

Serves: 2
Prep Time: 30 minutes

2 **young squirrels**   **dill**
  flour   **oregano**
  salt and pepper   **dry mustard**
  dried onions   **rosemary**
  celery seed

Cut squirrel into quarter sections. Put flour and a pinch of each spice in a paper sack. Put meat in sack and shake well. Remove meat from sack and cook in skillet with ½ inch hot grease for approximately 30 minutes or until done. Drain. Serve with biscuits and gravy.

Harold Roy
Champaign, Illinois

SOUTHERN FRIED RATTLESNAKE

Serves: varies
Prep Time: 1 hour

1 **fair sized rattlesnake (6-10 lbs.), preferably a Diamondback**
2 **cups flour**
3 **eggs, beaten**
4 **cups bread or cracker crumbs**
3 **cups oil**

Carefully remove bones from rattlesnake. Dredge pieces in flour, dip in eggs and cover wtih bread crumbs. Fry in very hot oil (deep fry). Serve as entree to old rattlesnake eaters or as appetizers to initiates.

Walter Allen
Montgomery, Alabama

COUNTRY FRIED SQUIRREL

Serves: 3
Prep Time: 2 hours

2 squirrels, dressed	⅛ tsp. pepper
2 quarts water	4 T. butter or oleo
1 small onion, chopped	4 T. cornstarch
2 tsp. baking soda	¼ cup water
1 tsp. salt	

Cut squirrels into serving pieces. Add squirrels and baking soda to water and cook for three minutes. Draw off water and then rinse the squirrels in clean water and drain again. Add clean water, onion, salt and pepper. Cook until done, approximately 1½ to 2 hours.

Remove squirrels from broth and fry in butter or oleo for five minutes or until light brown. You can make squirrel gravy out of the broth by mixing 4 T. cornstarch with ¼ cup water then adding to the broth, stir until thick.

Frederick Stites
Onsted, Michigan

SQUIRREL PIE

Serves: 3-4
Prep Time: 2 hours

  1 **squirrel**
  3 **T. flour**
  ½ **T. minced parsley**
  1 **tsp. salt**
  ⅛ **tsp. pepper**
  ½ **cup fresh mushrooms**
  2 **cups stock or milk**
  2 **cups flour**
  4 **tsp. baking powder**
  ½ **tsp. salt**
  ¼ **cup fat**
  ⅔ **cup milk**

Cut squirrel into two or three pieces. Cover with water and
cook one hour. Remove meat from bones in large pieces.
Add flour, parsley, salt, pepper and mushrooms to stock.
Cook until it thickens, five to 10 minutes. Add the meat
and mix well. Pour into baking dish.Make the pie crust by
sifting flour, baking powder and salt together. Cut in the
fat and add the milk. Stir until all dry ingredients are
moistened. Roll only enough to make it fit the baking
dish. Place dough on meat in baking dish. Bake in 350 degree oven until dough is golden brown, 30 to 40 minutes.

Mark Layman
Wayne, Kentucky

CRITTER CASSEROLE

Serves: 6
Prep Time: 1 hour 45 minutes

> 1½ lbs. game meat, boned and cut into small cubes
>   3 medium carrots, sliced
>   3 stalks celery, sliced
>   1 medium onion, diced
>   1 6 oz. can mushroom pieces (drain and save juice)
>   1 can cream of mushroom soup
>   1 cup rice
>   ¼ tsp. each onion salt, paprika and celery salt
>   1 tsp. parsley
>   2 T. each butter, flour and cooking oil
>   salt and pepper

Roll meat in flour, brown in oil. Drain oil and set aside. In sauce pan, put rice and 1¾ cup cold water, bring to boil, cover and remove from heat. Put carrots in pan, cover with water and boil until they start to get tender. Drain and set aside.

In 10-inch frying pan, saute onions, celery and mushrooms in butter for 10 minutes on low heat. Add carrots and meat, remove from heat. Add rice, mushroom juice, soup and seasonings. Mix thoroughly. Pour into greased 2-quart casserole dish, sprinkle with paprika. Bake in preheated oven for one hour, 15 minutes at 325 degrees. This can be used with any game and it comes out tasting great.

Roger Vass
Red Feather Lakes, Colorado

DOVE ENCHILADAS

Serves: 4
Prep Time: 2½ hours

  8 dove breasts
  1 doz. corn tortillas
    cheddar cheese, grated
Sauce:
  1 can mushroom soup   **½ cup onion, chopped**
  1 soup can of milk   **and sauteed**
    chopped fresh mushrooms **4 oz. green pepper**
    salt and pepper   **chopped**

Boil dove breasts until tender. When they cool, bone and cut the dove meat into ¼-inch cubes. Prepare the sauce. Add the dove meat to the sauce and bring all ingredients slowly to a boil. Cover and simmer for one hour.

Cover the bottom of a 9 x 13-inch pan with four tortillas. Cover with approximately ¼ of the sauce and add grated cheese. Repeat the process two more times to construct three tiers. The third layer should use the remaining sauce and should fill the dish enough to cover the tortillas completely. The final layer of cheese should be thicker than the first two layers.

Cover pan with foil and bake for 30 minutes at 350 degrees. Remove foil and bake for an additional 20 to 30 minutes.

Michael D. Arehart
Penn Laird, Virginia

DOVE IN A BLANKET

Serves: 4
Prep Time: 30-45 minutes

**16 doves, cleaned
 8 strips bacon, cut in half
 8 jalapeno peppers
    salt and pepper
    Worcestershire sauce
    butter**

Line a 3-inch baking pan with foil to retain juices. Place ½ jalapeno pepper inside each bird cavity. Season tops of birds with salt and pepper. Wrap each bird with bacon strips and secure with toothpicks. Shake tops of birds with Worcestershire sauce and brush lightly with butter. Bake uncovered at 350 degrees until birds are done, about 20 minutes.

Serve with wild rice cooked with mushrooms. A burgundy or dry rose wine goes very well with this dinner.

Jennie Crowder
Johnson City, Texas

DOVE GUMBO FILÉ

Serves: 6
Prep Time: 1 hour

- **12 doves**
- **1 cup cooking oil**
- **2½ T. chopped parsley**
- **2½ cups chopped onion**
- **4 T. flour**
- **2 chopped green onion tops**
- **salt and pepper**
- **¼ tsp. filé powder**

Saute dove in cooking oil until brown. Remove dove and add flour to oil in pot. Stir and cook until flour is very brown. (In south Louisiana this is called a "roux".) Add onions and cook until tender. Return dove to pot, add 2½ quarts boiling water. Cook slowly until dove is done, adding seasoning when water is added. Just before serving, add onion tops and parsley. Serve over cooked rice in deep bowl. Add ¼ tsp. filé to each bowl when served.

Derwood Vendever
Lafayette, Louisiana

DOVE STROGANOFF

Serves: 4
Prep Time: 1 hour

- **12 doves**
- **12 slices bacon**
- **mushrooms, to taste**
- **1 cup cheddar cheese, shredded**
- **1 package homestyle egg noodles**
- **2 cans cream of mushroom soup**
- **¼ cup lemon juice**
- **1 cup rose wine (optional)**

Prepare doves. Marinate overnight in wine (optional). Wrap slice of bacon around each dove and secure with toothpick. Baste with lemon juice and water. Bake at 375 degrees for 30 minutes. Meanwhile, cook mushrooms, soup and egg noodles separately. When birds are tender, combine mushrooms, soup and noodles into pan with doves. Heat for 15 minutes. Top with cheese and pats of butter. Heat 15 minutes more and serve.

Alan Pearce
Seaford, Delaware

DOVE AND OYSTER PIE

Serves: 4-6
Prep Time: 2 hours

16 doves
2 cups celery, chopped
1 cup onion, chopped
3 slices bacon, chopped
salt
cayenne pepper
1 quart water
4 dozen oysters
4 T. flour
¼ cup water

Place cleaned, whole doves in heavy pot. Add celery, onion, bacon, salt and pepper and cover with water. Let water come to a boil, reduce heat and simmer until doves are tender. Remove from heat. Place birds on a flat pan until cool enough to handle. Drain oysters, then stuff as many oysters as possible into each dove. Mix flour with ¼ cup water to make paste, then add enough liquid from pot to blend well. Add this to the pot in which doves were cooked, put on low heat and stir constantly until thickened about the consistency of cream. Add the remaining oysters and remove from heat. Line deep casserole bottom and sides with flaky pastry and bake for about 10 minutes in 350 degree oven to set pastry. Remove from oven and let cool. Put in a layer of doves, then a layer of liquid with oysters. Repeat until casserole is within ½ inch of top. Cover with pastry rolled thin. Prick top of pastry and bake at 350 degrees.

Tom Michelson
Roanoke, Virginia

BARRAS JAMBALAYA

Serves: 10
Prep Time:

2 lbs. dove or quail meat	1 tsp. black pepper
1½ lbs. smoke sausage	¼ cup cooking oil
1 lb. shrimp	2 lbs. rice
2 cans stewed tomatoes	1 cup diced green onion
1 diced bell pepper	¼ tsp. garlic salt
1 cup diced onion	2 banana peppers, diced
1 tsp. salt	

Cook the wild game until done. Cook the sausage separately and dice when done. Debone the meat, then cut into one inch pieces. Put the tomato, bell peppers, onions, salt, black pepper, cooking oil, green onion, garlic salt and banana peppers into a dutch oven. Add the wild game and sausage. Add one quart of water and bring to a boil, then cook for 15 minutes. Add shrimp and cook for an additional 20 minutes. Wash the rice then add to pot. Add water to the pot so it covers the ingredients by one inch. Boil for five minutes, then cover pot and steam cook for 40 minutes in the oven at 250 degrees.

Dr. Donald Barras
Troy, Alabama

COOT 'N' GRAVY

Serves: 4
Prep Time: 24 hours

Marinade:
  2 cups burgundy or claret wine
  ¼ cup cider vinegar
  1 T. salt
  ¼ tsp. peppercorns
  1 bay leaf, whole
  1 medium onion, sliced
  1 carrot, sliced
  2 T. sugar
  3 whole cloves

Skin three or four coot and remove all fat. Soak in salt water for one hour, then soak in marinade overnight in a glass bowl. Drain the birds and put marinade on low heat. Brown birds in olive oil or butter, pouring marinade over birds a little at a time. Cook until fork tender.

Remove meat and add six or eight ginger snaps to liquid. Stir until they dissolve. Serve with crusty Italian or French bread.

Joe LaBarbera
Milwaukee, Wisconsin

COOT STEW

Serves: 2-4
Prep Time: 2½ hours

  2 **coots**
  6 **egg-sized onions**
  5 **carrots, cut in one-inch sections**
  5 **tomatoes, diced and peeled**
  1 **hefty pinch of marjoram**
  2 **T. parsley, chopped**
  1 **tsp. pepper**
  1 **T. salt**
  2 **bay leaves**
  1 **quart water**
  3 **T. wine or cider vinegar**

Skin the coots, removing all adhering fat, and cut out the breast, legs and thighs. Prepare a large pot (preferably of thick iron with a heavy cover) with the remaining ingredients. Salt and pepper the coots, dredge sections through flour and brown in a large skillet with butter. Put browned coot sections along with the butter gravy (thinned out with a little water) into pot with the vegetables and simmer very slowly with cover on, for about two hours or until coot is tender.

Steve Czerniak
Milwaukee, Wisconsin

FRIED MARSH HEN

Serves: 4
Prep Time: 2 hours

12 marsh hens	1 T. salt
3 cups Bisquick	1 T. pepper
1 lb. shortening	

Cut marsh hens into thirds, leaving breasts whole. Salt and pepper to taste. Place Bisquick and birds in large brown paper bag. Shake well. Be sure all birds are well covered with Bisquick. Fry in iron skillet, half filled with shortening, until brown. Make gravy with drippings and serve over rice.

George J. Osborne
Jacksonville, Florida

PHEASANT PARISIENNE

Serves: 3-4
Prep Time: 6-8 hours

1 pheasant, cut up salt, pepper paprika	1 4 oz. can mushroom slices
½ cup dry white wine	1 cup sour cream mixed with
1 can cream of mushroom soup	¼ cup flour

Sprinkle pheasant lightly with salt, pepper and paprika. Place in crock pot. Mix wine, soup and mushrooms, pour over pheasant. Sprinkle with paprika. Cover and cook on low 6 to 8 hours. Remove pheasant and stir in sour cream mixture during last 30 minutes. (Put pheasant back in.) Serve with rice or noodles. Sauce makes great gravy.

Eugene Fletcher
Lebanon, New Jersey

PHEASANT EN CREME

Serves: 8
Prep Time: 2-3 hours

4 **pheasants**	1 **cup dry sherry**
4 **cans cream of**	2 **tsp. tarragon leaves**
chicken soup	2 **T. Worcestershire**
2 **cups light cream**	

Cut pheasants in half or section; wash and pat dry. Shake pieces in bag with a little seasoned flour to coat. Brown lightly in butter and a little oil. Arrange in shallow baking pan, cut side down. Combine undiluted soup with remaining ingredients in skillet used for browning. Heat and stir until smooth. Pour over pheasant; sprinkle with paprika. Bake uncovered in 350 degree oven 1½-2 hours or until fork-tender. Baste several times with the sauce during baking. Sprinkle once more with paprika. Arrange on heated platter, garnish with parsley bouquets, arrange sauteed mushroom caps over top (optional). Pass gravy in bowl.

Avis Roe
Golden Valley, Minnesota

PHEASANT WITH APPLES

Serves: 4-6
Prep Time: 1½ hours

¼ **cup flour**	**Saute:**
1 **tsp. salt**	2 **apples**
¼ **tsp. pepper**	3 **T. butter**
2 **pheasants, cut up**	1 **tsp. sugar**
6 **T. butter**	
4 **cups sauterne**	
¾ **cup light cream**	
3 **egg yolks**	

Combine flour, salt and pepper in a plastic bag. Add pheasant pieces and shake to coat. Brown pheasant lightly in butter. Place pheasant and wine in dish, bake covered at 350 degrees for about one hour or until tender. Remove pheasant to warm platter. Beat cream with egg yolks, slowly stir into pan drippings. Cook and stir over medium heat just until sauce is smooth and thickened. Do not boil. Pour sauce over pheasant. Garnish platter with sauteed apples.

Sauteed apples: core and slice two apples into wedges. Put 3 T. butter in skillet and add apples. Sprinkle with 1 tsp. sugar and cook, turning often until lightly browned.

Tony Craven
Des Moines, Iowa

MOIST GROUSE WITH RICE

Serves: 4
Prep Time: 15 minutes

- **4 breasts of grouse**
- **1 can peas**
- **1 can chicken broth**
  - **water**
  - **salt and pepper**
- **1 cup cooked rice (not Minute Rice)**
  - **poultry seasoning**
  - **parsley**
  - **sliced mushrooms**

Preheat oven to 350 degrees. In shallow baking dish, place peas, including canned water. Add can of chicken broth with enough water to make two cups. Spread rice across evenly, topping with sliced mushrooms. Season grouse breasts with salt, pepper, poultry seasoning and place across mixture in baking dish. Sprinkle entire thing with a little more salt, pepper and poultry seasoning and some dry parsley. Cover with foil and bake for one hour.

John Robinson
Coopersburg, Pennsylvania

SWEET AND SOUR SNOW GOOSE

Serves: 2
Prep Time: 3 hours

1 goose, skinned	3 apples, diced
1 jar sweet & sour sauce	2 apples, halved
1 can crushed pineapple	1 orange, diced
1 can ring pineapple	

Heat oven to 275 degrees. Place sweet and sour sauce, crushed pineapple, diced apples, diced orange into bowl. Using all juices from pineapple ingredients, mix thoroughly. Stuff cavity with apple halves. Place goose into a covered roaster, baste generously every half hour or as often as necessary to prevent drying out. Last half hour place rings of pineapple on top of goose.

Tommy Everman
Iowa Falls, Iowa

FORGOTTEN BIRDS

Serves: 2-4
Prep Time: 2½ hours

1½ cups raw rice
3½ lbs. grouse, ducks or other birds
  1 package onion soup mix
  1 can cream of mushroom soup
  3 cups boiling water

Pour rice into buttered roaster. Combine soup and water and pour over rice. Sprinkle with dry soup mix. Cover with foil and bake 2½ hours at 350 degrees.

David Hernesmaa
Ely, Minnesota

SALTED QUAIL EGGS

Serves: 15
Prep Time: 1 hour

100 eggs	**¼ cup table salt**
5 cups water	**2 tsp. monosodium glutamate**

Place eggs in water, bring to a boil and boil for three to four minutes. Remove eggs and rinse in warm water. Add ingredients to boiling water, making sure salt dissolves.

Do not shell eggs, place in quart jars and add salt water while hot. Let it cool and keep refrigerated. Ready to use after five days. Shell eggs and serve as hors d'oeuvres or as salad trimmings.

Watson T. Yoshimoto
Honolulu, Hawaii

GAMBEL QUAIL

Serves: varies
Prep Time: 45 minutes

enough quail for every-one, cut in pieces	**butter**
flour	**½ cup oil**
salt and pepper	**½ cup cooking sherry**

Roll breast and legs in flour, salt and pepper. Put butter and oil into electric skillet set at 350 degrees. Cook until browned. After quail is browned, set at 250 degrees, pour ½ cup cooking sherry into skillet and simmer for 20 minutes. Drippings in pan make excellent gravy.

Gary Spitler
Las Vegas, Nevada

BAKED QUAIL

Serves: 4-6
Prep Time: 1 hour 15 minutes

6 quail	¼ cup butter
4 T. Worcestershire	2 T. molasses
½-1 T. olive oil	salt and pepper
juice of three lemons	1 tsp. prepared mustard

Put quail in roasting pan with enough water to cover bottom of the pan. Cover and place in 300 degree oven. Combine other ingredients and blend together over low heat. When quail have cooked for 30 minutes, remove from oven, pour sauce over, cover and continue cooking 35 minutes longer, basting frequently. During last 10 minutes of cooking time, remove cover to brown birds and thicken sauce.

Jeff Hunt
Orange Park, Florida

ROAST MALLARD DUCK

Serves: 2-4
Prep Time: 45 minutes

1-1½ lbs. duck	**½ pared, cored apple**
1½ tsp. salt	**1 small peeled onion**
½ tsp. pepper	**2 thin slices salt pork**

Sprinkle body cavity of duck with ½ tsp. salt. Sprinkle remainder of the salt and pepper on the outside of the body. Place apple and onion in body cavity. Truss bird and place on rack in an uncovered baking pan. Lay the slices of salt pork over the breast. Place bird in a very hot oven (500 degrees) for 18 to 20 minutes (rare). If you use a 350 degree oven and wish the bird well-done, plan on 15 to 20 minutes per pound. Baste frequently with the drippings. Gravy may be made from the drippings in the pan. Duck may be stuffed with wild rice stuffing, if desired.

WILD RICE STUFFING

½ cup wild rice	**½ tsp. sage**
1 quart boiling water	**dash thyme**
salt and pepper	**1 T. melted fat**
½ lb. fresh mushrooms, sauteed	**1 egg yolk, beaten**

Cook rice in boiling water until tender, approximately 25 minutes. Drain and rinse. Add remaining ingredients and blend well. Will fill a 2-pound bird.

Richard Kempf
Woodville, Pennsylvania

CREAM OF MUSHROOM DUCK

Serves: 2-4
Prep Time: 2½ hours

6 boneless duck breasts, halved
flour
salt and pepper
1 onion
1 can cream of mushroom soup

Salt and pepper breast halves, roll in flour and brown in frying pan. Place in 2-inch deep baking dish and bake at 350 degrees for one hour.

Dice and saute one onion, mix with one can cream of mushroom soup. Pour over duck breasts and bake for one more hour.

Barbara McCoy
Glide, Oregon

MUSHROOM MALLARDS

Serves: 4
Prep Time: 2½ hours

2	large mallards	⅓	cup white wine
	salt and pepper	1	small onion
	poultry seasoning		mushrooms
	sage		gravy (flour and water)
1½	cups chicken broth	½	tsp. Kitchen Bouquet

Season ducks with salt, pepper, sage and poultry seasoning. In a small roaster put broth, wine, onions, ducks and
mushrooms. Cover and bake at 325 degrees until birds are
tender. Remove birds ½ hour before serving and make
gravy from juices. Replace birds in gravy, bake ½ hour
more. Serve with steamed broccoli and mashed potatoes.

Joni Millsop
Grand Forks, North Dakota

STUFFED CANADA GEESE

Serves: 4-6
Prep Time: 24 hours

1-2 **Canada geese**
     salt and pepper
     garlic powder
     onion powder
3-4 **cups water**
  1 **large can mushrooms (do not drain)**
1-2 **packages Lipton's Onion Soup Mix (dry)**

Season geese liberally with salt, pepper, garlic and onion powder inside and out. Place three to four cups of water in roasting pan. Make your favorite sage and onion stuffing and stuff birds. Put birds in pan, breast side up. Add can of mushrooms and juice. Sprinkle one to two packages Lipton's Onion Soup Mix over birds. Roast for 2 to 2½ hours at 325 degrees the day before serving. Make lots of gravy from juice. Slice all meat from bones when cold, put in gravy in roasting pan. Save some gravy for reheating stuffing. When ready to serve, reheat geese in gravy for 1½ to 2 hours in oven at 250 degrees along with stuffing and enjoy.

Bill Minta
East Troy, Wisconsin

MOUNTAIN STATE TURKEY STROGANOFF

Serves: 6
Prep Time: 1 hour

    4 cups white and dark turkey meat (cooked)
   12 oz. turkey gravy
   ¾ cup milk
   ½ cup green pepper, chopped
   ½ cup onion, chopped
    1 can mixed vegetables
    1 can mushroom soup
    1 tsp. salt
   ¼ tsp. pepper
   ½ tsp. celery seed
    1 cup water
    1 4 oz. pkg. shredded mild cheddar cheese

Preheat oven to 325 degrees. Put turkey meat, milk,
mushroom soup and gravy into a cooking pan and heat until warm. In another cooking pan add mixed vegetables,
salt, pepper, celery seed, green pepper, onion and water;
cook five to ten minutes. Drain water and combine in a
baking dish, add cheddar cheese on top and bake until
cheese melts and serve.

Kenneth W. Crummett
Moyers, West Virginia

ROAST WILD TURKEY

Serves: 4-6

1 wild turkey, dressed	**1 cup sherry**
1 T. pepper	**½ T. salt**
4 strips bacon	

To prepare for roasting, wipe turkey clean inside and out with a damp cloth. Stuff with stuffing, truss, salt and pepper, then place four strips of bacon on breast. Roast uncovered for one hour at 325-350 degrees. After the first hour, soak a heavy paper towel with sherry and place over bird. Baste every ten minutes with drippings. Most wild turkeys weigh from eight to fifteen pounds dressed. Roast 15-20 minutes per pound. Baste frequently.

Russell Browning
Santa Rosa, California

CREAMY HEART STROGANOFF

Serves: 2-4
Prep Time: 2½-3 hours

- 2 hearts
- 3 cups water
- 1 large onion, diced
- 6 fresh mushrooms, diced
- 1 stalk celery, diced
- 1 can creamy chicken mushroom soup
- ½ cup sour cream
- 1 cup broth (heart, chicken or turkey)
- 3 T. Butter Flavored Crisco
- ½ tsp. salt

Place hearts in kettle with three cups water and ½ tsp. salt. Cook until tender. Melt Crisco in skillet. Saute onion, celery and mushrooms. Dice the precooked heart and add broth and meat to skillet. Stir over low heat until heated through. Add soup and sour cream. Stir over low heat until heated through. Serve over rice or egg noodles.

Note: For added flavor, use chicken or turkey broth in place of heart broth.

Thomas Grimes
Westminster, Maryland

WILD RABBIT WITH WINE

1½ lb. dressed rabbit
  2 tsp. salt
  ¼ tsp. pepper
  3 T. butter
  3 T. flour
  ½ cup onion, minced
  ½ cup canned mushrooms
  ½ tsp. thyme
  1 T. parsley
  1 bay leaf, crumbled
  ½ cup red wine
  ½ cup mushroom liquid
  2 cups water

Brown the rabbit pieces in butter (you may dredge pieces with flour). Remove rabbit from pan and add onions and mushrooms. More butter may be needed also. When onion is soft and slightly brown, push onions and mushrooms to one side and add the flour. Mix thoroughly, then add the water, mushroom liquid, wine and seasonings. Place the pieces of rabbit in the pan and cover. Steam for 1½ hours or until tender.

Tanya Brown
Weston, Ohio

GAME SAUSAGE CASSEROLE

Serves: 4
Prep Time: 1¼ hours

1 lb. game sausage	1 cup instant rice
1 cup celery, chopped	(white/brown/wild)
1 large onion, chopped	1 pkg. onion soup mix
5 cups water	

Brown sausage, celery and onion, then drain off fat. Mix all ingredients together in baking dish and bake one hour at 350 degrees.

Note: Big, small or upland game meat may be used with this recipe.

Michael D. Ferrin
Lyman, Wyoming

FRICASSEED RACCOON

Serves: 8
Prep Time: 2 hours

1 raccoon, cut in pieces	1 cup flour
2 T. salt	¼ cup fat
½ tsp. pepper	2 cups broth

Rub raccoon pieces with salt and pepper and roll in flour. Cook in hot fat until brown. Add the broth, cover and simmer for two hours or until tender.

Carl Engle
Fostoria, Kansas

BAKED BEAVER OR RACCOON

Serves: 2-4
Prep Time: 2½ hours

    1 **beaver or raccoon, skinned and defatted**
       salt and pepper
       garlic powder
       celery top from one rib of celery
    1 **onion, peeled**
    2 **carrots, peeled**
    ½ **cup brandy**
    2 **cups water**

Season the meat with salt, pepper and garlic powder.
Place in a roast pan with celery tops, onion and carrots.
Bake, covered, at 350 degrees for one hour. Add the brandy
and water. Bake one hour and 15 minutes longer. Baste
occasionally with the liquid in pan.

Mike McKenzie
Yukon, Canada

FRIED BEAVER TAIL

Serves: 2
Prep Time: 30 minutes (plus soaking time)

2 **beaver tails**
cold water
½ **cup vinegar**
1 **T. salt**
2 **tsp. baking soda**
2 **quarts water**
½ **tsp. salt**
¼ **tsp. pepper**
¼ **cup flour**
¼ **cup butter**
½ **cup dry sherry**
1 **tsp. dry mustard**
1 **tsp. sugar**
¼ **tsp. garlic powder**
1 **T. Worcestershire sauce**

Skin the beaver tails, clean thoroughly. Let soak overnight in cold water, add vinegar and 1 T. salt to the water. Remove the tails from the brine. Rinse in cold water. Add baking soda to the two quarts water. Add the beaver tails. Bring to a boil, reduce heat and simmer for 10 minutes. Drain and rinse. Season tails with salt and pepper and dredge in flour. Saute in butter until tender. Mix the sherry, mustard, sugar, garlic powder and Worcestershire sauce together. Add to the beaver tails and simmer very gently for about 10 minutes, basting frequently. Slice and serve.

Paul Siebert
Portland, Oregon

ABOUT THE CHEF

Scott Ekenberg knows what it takes to create delicious wild game dinners. He's not only an experienced hunter and established chef, but he now also has three wild game cookbooks under his belt.

Before taking on the duties of Executive Chef at Olympic Hills Golf Club in Eden Prairie, Minnesota, Scott studied and worked from San Francisco to New York, but he is most comfortable in the game-rich Midwest, where his free time is spent afield with fellow North American Hunting Club members. Scott has received recognition for his culinary talents by The White House, members of Congress and the House of Representatives. Even so, he is most at home when he can trade in his chef's hat for a hunting cap and his white coat for a camouflage parka.

Scott was winning gold medals in national cooking competitions before he even entered the famed Culinary Institute of America.

For years Scott has hunted with NAHC staffers and members. And when Scott is preparing dinner back at camp, it's not easy to stay out until the end of shooting hours. Whether he's next to the campfire or in the kitchen, the first question at the end of a hunting day is not, "What did you see today?" It's "What's cooking for supper?"

GOURMET MEALS

WILD GOBBLER SUPPER

MENU

Romaine Salad Mimosa

Wild Turkey Croquettes

Simple Trifle

Recommended wine:
Zinfandel

WILD TURKEY CROQUETTES

Serves: 4-6
Prep Time: 1 hour

2 ribs celery, chopped
1 small onion, chopped
1/8 lb. melted butter
1 cup flour
2 cups heavy cream
4 cups cooked turkey meat, chopped fine
2 sprigs parsley
salt and white pepper

Breading:
2 eggs
2 cups bread crumbs
flour

Mix all ingredients in a large bowl until a very heavy dough is formed. Now shape into large meatballs. Roll in flour, dip in egg and roll in bread crumbs. Now deep fry in oil until golden brown. Serve with your favorite cream gravy. Goes well with fresh fruit garnish.

ROMAINE SALAD MIMOSA

Serves: 4
Prep Time: 15 minutes

1 head romaine	**Dressing:**
8 large fresh mushrooms	1 cup cider vinegar
4 hard boiled eggs	salt, white pepper
½ can chopped beets	2 cups salad oil
	(walnut oil is best)

Wash and core the romaine, cut lengthwise to make four sections. Open the sections up on a salad plate. Garnish the romaine with the mushrooms, sliced thin. Sprinkle over the chopped hard boiled eggs, then the drained, chopped beets. Top with the dressing.

SIMPLE TRIFLE

Serves: 4
Prep Time: 15 minutes

There are no quantities to this recipe. The amount you make depends on how many calories you want!

pound cake	strawberry preserves
whipped cream	sherry to taste
blueberries	toasted almonds

In a glass dish or bowl layer the ingredients. Crumble pound cake, then sprinkle with sherry, dollop with strawberry preserves, then whipped cream, blueberries and toasted almonds. You can repeat this layering as many times as you want.

LIGHT-N-SPICY DINING

MENU

Vegetable Salad

Quails with Pecan Butter Sauce

Grape Tart

Recommended wine:
Rosé

VEGETABLE SALAD

Serves: 4
Prep Time: 30 minutes

1 **large carrot, chopped**
2 **cups green beans, blanched and cut**
1 **cup green peas (frozen type)**
2 **ribs celery, diced**
1 **small jar pimentos, diced**
1 **small can kidney beans, drained**
   broccoli florettes from one head of broccoli
   mayonnaise to taste

Put all ingredients in a bowl. Mix with mayonnaise to the
desired consistency. Serve in a lettuce cup. You may want
to sprinkle the top with brown sugar.

QUAILS WITH PECAN BUTTER SAUCE

Serves: 2
Prep Time: 45 minutes

4-6 quails, deboned	**½ tsp. lemon juice**
salt and white pepper	**½ clove garlic**
4 T. butter	**1 shot Tabasco**
¼ cup pecans	**1 shot Worcestershire**
1 T. onions	

Bone out quails, season with salt and pepper and saute in 2 T. butter. Mix the remaining ingredients in a blender until creamy. Put mixture over quails and finish in the oven.

GRAPE TART

Serves: 8
Prep Time: 40 minutes

1 pie shell	**Pastry Cream:**
seedless grapes	**1½ cups milk**
1 cup apricot preserves	**4 egg yolks**
½ cup water	**¼ cup flour**
	½ cup sugar
	1 capful vanilla

For pastry cream, scald the milk and vanilla. In a double boiler mix the yolks, flour, sugar and cook until smooth and creamy. Cool.

To make the tart: fill pie shell with pastry cream. Arrange grapes on top to cover the whole pie. Heat the preserves and water to a boil. Strain and brush over grapes. Chill until the apricot is set.

SAUCE FOR THE GOOSE...

MENU

Cucumber Salad

Wild Goose With Apple Sauce

Rice Custard

Recommended wine:
Brut Champagne

WILD GOOSE WITH APPLE SAUCE

Serves: 4-6
Prep Time: 4 hours

1 large goose
  salt and pepper
2 cups apple juice
3 large apples
  cored and diced
1 tsp. cinnamon

4 cloves
  juice of 1 lemon
½ tsp. nutmeg
2 T. butter
½ cup raisins

Season the goose with salt and pepper; roast in a pre-heated oven at 350 degrees for two hours. Let cool slightly then take all meat and skin off bones and cut into strips. Now put the strips and all the other ingredients in a casserole dish, and bake for 45 minutes at 350 degrees. Serve with white rice.

CUCUMBER SALAD

Serves: 4
Prep Time: 15 minutes

2 cucumbers, sliced thin
1 T. salt
½ cup sugar
1 cup apple cider vinegar

½ onion, sliced thin
1 T. dill
1½ cups sour cream
chives (garnish)

Mix the salt with the cucumbers, put in a covered bowl
and refrigerate for 10 minutes. Pour off any liquid, add all
ingredients and mix well. Serve on a bed of lettuce.

RICE CUSTARD

Serves: 4-6
Prep Time: 2 hours

4 egg yolks
2 cups boiled rice
2 cups heavy cream
1 cup sugar

1 capful of vanilla
1 tsp. nutmeg
cinnamon and brown
sugar to sprinkle

Combine first six ingredients, put in custard cups and
bake in a pan of water at 325 degrees for one hour. Chill
and unmold, then sprinkle with cinnamon and brown
sugar.

SUNNY SUNDAY BRUNCH

MENU

Sliced Tomato Vinaigrette

Venison Breakfast Hash

Baked Apple Streusel

Recommended wine:
Beaujolais

VENISON BREAKFAST HASH

Serves: 4
Prep Time: 35 minutes

1¼ lb. cooked venison steak, finely diced
¼ lb. bacon, diced
½ onion, diced
2 potatoes, cooked and diced
⅛ lb. butter
    salt and white pepper

Mix all ingredients except for butter; melt butter in a pan.
Add hash mixture to butter and fry until golden brown
and crisp. Top it with poached eggs. For brunch serve with
sliced tomato salad. Also works well with moose.

SLICED TOMATO VINAIGRETTE

4 tomatoes	Vinaigrette:
6 green onions, chopped	1 cup cider vinegar
½ head lettuce	salt and white pepper
	2 cups salad oil
	pinch each:
	marjoram
	sweet basil
	chopped parsley
	chopped garlic

Mix vinaigrette ingredients and chill. Dress the plates with lettuce leaves, top with sliced tomatoes. Sprinkle the green onion on top and spoon dressing over all.

BAKED APPLE STREUSEL

Serves: 4
Prep Time: 1 hour 20 minutes

3 apples cored, peeled and sliced
½ lemon (juice only)
¼ cup butter
¼ cup sugar
½ cup flour
cinnamon to taste

Put the apples in baking dish and sprinkle the lemon juice over them. Mix the butter, sugar, flour and cinnamon. Sprinkle mixture over the apples and bake at 325 degrees for one hour.

COZY FIRESIDE FARE

MENU

Hot German Slaw

Rabbit with Cherry Sauce

Caramel Custard

Recommended wine:
Vouvray

RABBIT WITH CHERRY SAUCE

Serves: 4
Prep Time: 1 hour

> 1 **rabbit, cut up**
>   **salt and white pepper**
>   **flour for dredging**
> 1/8 **lb. butter**
> 1 **can bing cherries with juice**
> 1½ **cups cherry flavored brandy**
> 2 **T. cornstarch**
>   **nutmeg (optional)**

Season the rabbit with salt and pepper, dredge in flour
and fry in butter until brown. Pour off grease. Add brandy
away from flame, light with a match. Let flame, return to
fire and add the cherries and juice. Dissolve the cornstarch
in a little water, add to the rabbit. Bring to a boil and simmer slowly for 40 minutes. Serve with sage dressing.

HOT GERMAN SLAW

Serves: 6-10
Prep Time: 15 minutes

- ¼ lb. bacon, diced
- 2 oz. cider vinegar
- 1 small head cabbage, shredded
- ½ small onion, chopped
- 3 T. sugar
  salt and white pepper to taste

Brown the bacon and add the vinegar. Mix with all other ingredients. Garnish with fresh chives and serve warm.

CARAMEL CUSTARD

Serves: 4
Prep Time: 2 hours

- ½ cup sugar
- ¼ cup water
- 4 egg yolks
- 3 cups heavy cream
- 1 cup sugar
- 1 capful vanilla

Mix the ½ cup sugar and ¼ cup water in a sauce pan and carmelize. Pour this into custard cups. Mix the remaining ingredients and pour into cups. Bake in a pan with about one inch of water in a 325 degree oven for one hour. When done, flip cups onto plate and chill. After chilled remove from cup. If they are still sticking, cut around the edges.

SAVORY SUMMER TREAT

MENU

Fresh Fruit Compote

Pheasant Curry

Poached Pear With Raspberry Sauce

Recommended wine:
Piesporter

PHEASANT CURRY

Serves: 2
Prep Time: 40 minutes

2 large pheasant breasts flour for dredging	1 T. chopped chili peppers
Seasoning:	1 tomato, diced
2 T. curry powder	1 banana, sliced
½ tsp. sweet basil	1 apple, cored and
½ tsp. black pepper	diced
½ tsp. cinnamon	2 T. raisins
1 tsp. cayenne pepper	2 T. chopped pecans
½ tsp. garlic powder	2 T. coconut
½ tsp. white pepper	2 T. butter
½ tsp. salt	1½ cups cream

Debone pheasant breasts and dredge in flour, then melt butter in skillet. Mix all spices, put pheasant breasts in hot butter and season with the spices, then fry until brown. Add all other ingredients and simmer for 10 to 15 minutes. Serve with rice.

FRESH FRUIT COMPOTE

Serves: 8-10
Prep Time: 25 minutes

All fruit must be fresh.

1 cantaloupe	juice of each:
1 honeydew	1 lemon
1 pint strawberries	1 lime
½ pint grapes	1 orange
½ pint cherries	
½ cup sugar	
1 small pineapple	
1 cup mayonnaise	
1 cup whipped cream (lightly sweetened)	

Dice all fruit, pit the cherries and dehull the strawberries.
Sprinkle the sugar over fruit, then squeeze the juice of the
lemon, line and orange over fruit and put in compote
glasses. Mix the whipped cream and the mayonnaise
together and put a dollop on each compote.

POACHED PEAR WITH RASPBERRY SAUCE

Serves: 4
Prep Time: 1 hour

4 pears, peeled and cored	Raspberry sauce:
2 cups white wine	1 lb. raspberries
½ lemon (juice only)	1 cup water
¼ cup sugar	2 cups sugar
½ cinnamon stick	1 shot Grande Marnier

Combine first five ingredients in a sauce pan and poach
pears until tender. Then chill in the poaching syrup. Next
combine all sauce ingredients and boil, then puree in
blender. Pour over chilled pears.

PATIO LUNCH OLE!

MENU

Gazpacho

Venison Taco Salad

Mexican Ice Cream

Recommended wine:
Spanish Red Wine

VENISON TACO SALAD

Serves: 4
Prep Time: 20 minutes

4 taco shells, large—
deep fried into bowl shape
½ head shredded lettuce
1 bag shredded cheddar
1 diced tomato
1 diced green pepper
1 diced small onion
sour cream
picante sauce

Meat Filling:
1 lb. ground venison
salt and pepper
½ tsp. chili powder
1 chopped garlic clove
½ tsp. paprika
½ tsp. cayenne pepper

Combine all meat filling ingredients in a skillet and brown. Assemble the salad by putting shredded lettuce in taco shell. Add warm meat filling, cheddar cheese, onion, green pepper, tomato, picante sauce and dollop of sour cream.

Note: Salad may be served in regular bowl with taco chips served on the side.

GAZPACHO

Serves: 10-12
Prep Time: 25 minutes

½ onion
1 green pepper
1 cucumber
1 tomato
2 cloves garlic
1 tsp. salt
1 tsp. pepper
    pinch cayenne
    pepper
    pinch thyme
    pinch savory
1 small can tomato puree
1 T. red wine vinegar
2 T. olive oil
½ lemon (juice only)
1 egg
6 oz. tomato juice

Combine all ingredients in a blender. Serve very cold.

MEXICAN ICE CREAM

Serves: 4
Prep Time: 5 minutes

4 large scoops vanilla ice cream
2 cups peanuts, chopped
1 cup coconut, shredded
    chocolate syrup

Roll scoops of ice cream in the chopped peanuts and coconut. Serve on top of chocolate syrup.

HEARTY HUNTERS FEAST

MENU

Wild Game and Cranberry Salad

Venison and Leek Pie

Apple Junkit

Recommended wine:
Cabernet Sauvignon

VENISON AND LEEK PIE

Serves: 4
Prep Time: 1 hour

1 pkg. pie dough	¼ tsp. cayenne pepper
1¼ lbs. leeks, sliced thin	1 T. chopped garlic
4 T. butter	1 T. paprika
1¼ lbs. ground venison	3 eggs
salt and pepper	¾ cup sour cream

Line a pie dish with dough. Brown the venison in butter and season with salt, pepper, cayenne, garlic and paprika. When brown add the leeks and cook until they are translucent. Cool this mixture slightly and mix in the eggs and sour cream. Pour in pie dish and bake in a 450 degree oven for about 10 minutes, then reduce heat to 300 degrees for ½ hour.

WILD GAME AND CRANBERRY SALAD

Serves: 4
Prep Time: 10 minutes

2 T. butter	1 cup salad oil
2 cups cranberries	1 head of chickory
¾ cup sugar	4 cups diced, cooked
1 cup apple cider vinegar	game

Wash chickory and put on four salad plates. Heat butter,
then add cranberries and cook until skin just splits. Add
sugar and stir for 30 seconds, then add vinegar and oil.
Add the cooked game and spoon over chickory.

APPLE JUNKIT

Serves: 4
Prep Time: 20 minutes

3 large Red Delicious	3 cloves
apples	½ tsp. nutmeg
12 oz. apple juice	3 T. sugar
½ lemon (juice only)	milk or heavy cream
½ stick cinnamon	

Decore and quarter the apples. Place in a sauce pan, cover
with remaining ingredients, cover pan and cook until
softened. Remove cinnamon stick, then mash mixture
until it has a smooth texture. Place in a bowl while still
warm and pour a little milk or heavy cream over top.

THE TASTE OF EXPERIENCE!

We received so many Hunting Reports from NAHC members with great comments about the camp food that we decided to ask some of these guides to share their favorite wild game recipes so that all the NAHC members could sample their great cooking. That's what we did — and the results were well worth it.

The guides and outfitters we asked responded generously, and now their camp feasts are yours to try. All of the recipes come from guides and outfitters that you have told us were the best. They're all NAHC recommended and approved, and we've even listed their addresses so you also have in your hands a mini-directory of guides and outfitters you know you can trust.

Some of the recipes are simple enough to be prepared at camp, as soon as you bring "the big one" in. Others are for savoring later with friends and family while you reminisce about your days afield. No matter which ones you choose to try, we're sure you'll enjoy this useful section.

GUIDES &
OUTFITTERS

RAGGED MOUNTAIN BUCKSKIN JERKY

Serves: 4
Prep Time: 24 hours

venison roast	**½ tsp. Tabasco sauce**
⅓ cup sugar	**½ tsp. onion powder**
¼ cup salt	**½ tsp. pepper**
2 cups soy sauce	**½ tsp. garlic powder**
1 cup red wine	**¼ tsp. liquid smoke**
1 tsp. Worcestershire	

Trim all fat from meat, slice with the grain about ¼ to ½-inch thick. (The meat slices better when semi-frozen.) Mix all ingredients together. Place meat in the cool brine and leave overnight or not less than eight hours. Remove from brine and air dry. Smoke in your smoker for 12 to 16 hours, checking for dryness and how you like it. I use three pansful of aspen (poplar) chips in the early part of the drying process.

Dion M. Luke
Ragged Mountain Outfitters, Inc.
1526 Blake
Glenwood Springs, CO 81601

MONTANA FRENCH DIP SANDWICHES

Serves: 5
Prep Time: 4½ hours

4-5 lbs. deer or antelope roast	4 stalks celery, minced
3 pkgs. Lipton Onion and Mushroom Soup mix	2-3 cups water

French Bread:

2 cups warm water	1 package yeast
2 tsp. salt	1 T. sugar
5¾ cups flour	

Combine ingredients for french bread buns, ending with flour. Use an electric mixer until too stiff, then knead until elastic. Place in a well oiled bowl and let rise for one hour. Divide into five equal portions and let rise five minutes. Gently knead into loaves about 6 inches long. Place on a greased cookie sheet. Cut each loaf ¾-inch deep and 1½-inch apart. Let rise just one hour (bread tends to fall if time is extended). Bake at 350 degrees about 20 minutes.

While bread is in first rising stage, place roast in a baking dish with two cups of water, celery and one package of soup. Sprinkle dry soup over meat. Add water if necessary during baking time. Bake at 300 to 325 degrees for 1½ hours or until done. Cool meat and slice wafer thin. Add to remaining stock two packages soup mix with water according to directions on package. Reserve and heat prior to serving with french dip sandwiches. Serve on a hot french bun sliced in half.

Mary Beth Kibler
Myron Kibler's Outfitting and Guide Service
Box A-6
Sand Springs, MT 59077

HAWAIIAN VENISON

Serves: 4
Prep Time: 20 minutes

- **1 lb. boneless venison round steak**
- **¼ cup flour**
- **¼ cup butter or margarine**
- **½ cup boiling water**
- **1 tsp. salt**
- **¼ cup sugar**
- **2-3 green peppers**
- **½ cup pineapple chunks**
- **2½ T. cornstarch**
- **½ cup pineapple juice**
- **¼ cup vinegar**
- **2½ T. soy sauce**

Cut steak into 1-inch cubes; dredge in flour. Brown meat in butter. Add water and salt; simmer until tender. Cut green peppers into 1-inch squares; boil 10 minutes and drain. Add peppers and pineapple chunks to meat. Combine remaining ingredients; cook until sauce is clear and thick. Pour sauce over meat mixture; simmer five minutes. Serve over chinese noodles or cooked rice. Garnish with chilled pineapple chunks.

Ruth Taggart
P & R Hunting Lodge
Rt. 5, Box 117
Dallas, SD 57529

BUCK AND BREAD

Serves: 8
Prep Time: 30 minutes

1 lb. ground venison	½ tsp. salt
½ cup chopped onion	½ tsp. basil
½ cup chopped ripe olives	⅛ tsp. pepper
4 cups buttermilk baking mix	2 T. parsley
mushroom sauce	1 egg yolk

Cook venison and onion until meat is browned. Remove from heat, stir in olives, salt, basil and pepper, set aside. In medium bowl, mix chopped parsley into baking mix. Quickly mix in ¾ cup cold water, just until mixture forms soft dough that leaves sides of bowl. Turn dough onto floured surface, knead eight to ten strokes. With rolling pin, lightly roll dough into 12 x 10-inch rectangle. Evenly spread cooled meat mixture on dough to within ½ inch of edges. Starting at narrow end, roll up dough, jelly-roll fashion. Tuck ends under. Place roll, seam side down on cookie sheet. Beat egg yolk with 1 T. water, brush roll with mixture. Bake at 425 degrees for 30 minutes or until browned. Meanwhile prepare mushroom sauce.

Mushroom sauce: Cook ½ lb. mushrooms in 2 T. butter and 1 beef bouillon cube until mushrooms are tender. In bowl, blend 1 T. flour with 1 cup water. Gradually stir into mushrooms, cook, stirring constantly until sauce is thickened. Slice roll and serve with sauce.

Dixie Luke
Ragged Mountain Outfitters, Inc.
1526 Blake
Glenwood Springs, CO 81601

WILD SWISS STEAK

Serves: 2-4
Prep Time: 1½ hours

2 lbs. round or roast, sliced 1-inch thick
½ medium onion, sliced
2 T. Worcestershire sauce
   dash pepper sauce
   dash garlic powder
   dash oregano leaves
   dash thyme
   dash celery seed
½ bay leaf
   dash tarragon leaves
   dash Italian seasoning
   salt and pepper
1 large can tomatoes, drained, save juice

Brown meat in shortening, add onion slices and finish
browning. Add tomatoes and spices. Cook for one hour or
more on low heat. Add tomato juice as needed. Serve over
rice.

Mr. Kim Bright
Boulder Lake Lodge
Box 1100
Pinedale, WY 82941

COOLWATER CHILI

Serves: 8-10
Prep Time: 3-4 hours

3½ lbs. ground venison
2 cups chopped celery
1½ cups diced onion
2 small cans diced green chilies
1 large can whole tomatoes
1 medium can whole tomatoes
3 cans tomato sauce
½ tsp. garlic powder
2 tsp. beef base
⅓ tsp. red pepper
¼ cup sugar
1 tsp. chili powder
1 tsp. cumin
 salt and pepper
 water

Brown meat and drain fat if necessary. Add all other ingredients in a large kettle and add water to desired consistency. Bring to a boil, reduce heat and simmer two to three hours, or cover and bake at 300 degrees for three to four hours.

Note: If at camp, you may chop your fresh game in small pieces and follow same recipe.

Shirley Wilson
Coolwater Outfitters
HCR #1, 98A
Kooskia, ID 83539

BARBEQUED MEATBALLS

Serves: 6-8
Prep Time: 1½ hours

3 lbs. ground elk, deer or moose
2 cups quick oats, uncooked
1 13 oz. can evaporated milk
1 cup chopped onion
2 eggs, beaten
2 tsp. salt
½ tsp. pepper
½ tsp. garlic powder
½ cup chopped onion
2 cups catsup
1½ cup brown sugar
1 T. liquid smoke
½ tsp. garlic powder

Lightly but thoroughly mix the first eight ingredients.
Shape into 1½-inch balls and place in a single layer in two
13 x 9-inch baking dishes. Combine catsup, brown sugar,
liquid smoke and garlic powder. Stir in the chopped onion.
Pour over the meatballs. Bake at 350 degrees for one hour.
Stir halfway through baking time.

Brenda Kuester
Rocky Point Outfitters
837 Swamp Creek Rd.
Plains, MT 59859

WILD GAME MINCE MEAT

Yield: 9 quarts
Prep Time: 2 hours

2 cups molasses	2 tsp. nutmeg
4 cups grape juice	2 lbs. currants
⅔ cup cider vinegar	2 tsp. allspice
8 T. butter	2 tsp. orange peel
3 lbs. elk or venison, boneless	2 tsp. ginger
4 tsp. cinnamon	2 cups brown sugar
2 lbs. raisins	1½ tsp. cloves
2 cups brown sugar	1 lemon rind and juice
	10-15 apples

Boil meat until tender in two cups water. Remove meat and run through a food chopper. Cut broth down to ¾ cup. Chop the apples. Mix the other ingredients and cook until fruit is tender. Freeze or can process 10 minutes at 10 lbs. pressure.

Dixie Luke
Ragged Mountain Outfitters, Inc.
1526 Blake
Glenwood Springs, CO 81601

HEARTY NACHOS

Serves: 8-10
Prep Time: 1½ hours

  1 2-lb. box of Velveeta cheese
  1 can cream of mushroom soup
  ½ lb. bacon, fried and crumbled
  1 8 oz. can tomatoes
  1 8 oz. can mushrooms
  2 lbs. ground meat (elk, deer, moose)
  1 tsp. pork sausage seasoning
  ¾ cup taco sauce

Brown and crumble the ground meat, season with the
pork sausage seasoning. Melt the cheese and add the remaining ingredients, including the meat mixture. This
can be done in a crock pot and kept warm for a party.
Serve as a dip or over lettuce and chips.

Brenda Kuester
Rocky Point Outfitters
837 Swamp Creek Rd.
Plains, MT 59859

CROCKPOT STEW IN CREAM GRAVY

Serves: 8
Prep Time: 8 hours

- 3 **lbs. stew meat (elk, moose, deer)**
- ¼ **cup flour**
- 2 **tsp. salt**
- ⅛ **tsp. paprika**
  fat for frying
- 8 **potatoes, peeled**
- 12 **carrots, peeled and sliced**
- 2 **thick onion slices**
- 1 **bay leaf**
- 1 **can cream of mushroom soup**
- 1 **cup sour cream**

Combine dry ingedients in a paper bag, shake stew pieces in flour mixture. Brown meat lightly in hot fat in heavy skillet. Remove meat to crock pot and add vegetables and the can of soup. Cover and stew on low for eight hours. Five minutes before serving, stir in sour cream and heat until warm. Serve hot.

Brenda Kuester
Rocky Point Outfitters
837 Swamp Creek Rd.
Plains, MT 59859

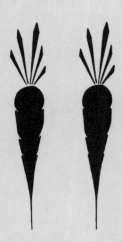

OLD FASHIONED NOODLE DINNER

Serves: 6-8
Prep Time: 2-3 hours

3-4 elk steaks	Noodles:
2-3 T. Crisco	2 eggs, beaten
2 beef bouillon cubes	1 tsp. salt
3 cups boiling water	3 T. milk
	2-2½ cups flour

Noodles: combine eggs, salt and milk. Add flour or enough to make stiff dough. Roll very thin. Let stand one hour. Roll up and slice ¼-inch wide. Unroll and let dry two to three hours.

Elk: cut steak from bone and then into strips. Brown in Crisco. Drain and add bouillon cubes and boiling water. Stir to dissolve cubes and then cover for two to three hours. Simmer until meat is tender. Drop dried noodles into three cups boiling salted water. Cook uncovered for 25 minutes. Add meat and liquid to cooked noodles and heat 10 minutes. Serve as is or over mashed potatoes.

Linda Baumeister
Lone Wolf Guide Service
Box 631
Livingston, MT 59047

STIR-FRY ELK

Serves: 6-8
Prep Time: 45 minutes

1½ lbs. boneless meat, cut in strips
¼ cup soy sauce
1 clove garlic, minced
¼ tsp. grated ginger root
   or ⅛ tsp. ground ginger
1½ cups carrot julienne strips
1½ cups broccoli, chopped
1 large green pepper, cut in strips or chunks
1 medium onion, cut in strips or chunks
3 T. oil
2 cups beef broth
3 T. cornstarch
   possible additions: cauliflower, mushrooms,
   bean sprouts, water chestnuts, bamboo sprouts

Mix soy sauce and meat, let stand while preparing vegetables. Put 2 T. of the oil in a wok with garlic and ginger. When hot, cook and stir meat until just cooked. Remove from wok, add the other T. of oil and start cooking vegetables. Begin with the firmest (carrots), cook and stir a couple minutes and then add broccoli. Cook and stir a couple more minutes and then add peppers, etc. Don't overcook; vegetables should be crisp. Add meat to vegetables in wok. Mix broth and cornstarch, pour over mixture in wok and cook and stir until thickened. Serve over rice.

Coralee McKee
Boulder Lake Lodge
Box 1100
Pinedale, WY 82941

SHOGUN ELK

Serves: 6
Prep Time: 30 minutes

- 1 **lb. boneless elk steak, cut ½-inch thick**
- 1 **small head cauliflower**
- 2 **T. butter**
- 1 **green pepper, cut in ¾-inch pieces**
- ¼ **cup soy sauce**
- 1 **clove garlic, minced**
- 2 **T. cornstarch**
- ½ **tsp. sugar**
- 1½ **cups beef broth or water**
- 1 **cup sliced green onion, with top**
- 3 **cups cooked rice**

Cut meat into ½-inch squares. Separate cauliflower into flowerettes (about four cups). Brown meat in butter about five minutes. Add cauliflower, green pepper, soy sauce and garlic. Stir lightly to coat vegetables with soy sauce. Cover pan and simmer until vegetables are barely tender (about 10 minutes). Blend cornstarch, sugar and beef broth. Add to meat mixture with green onions. Cook, stirring constantly until thoroughly heated and sauce is thickened. Serve over beds of fluffy rice.

Dixie Luke
Ragged Mountain Outfitters, Inc.
1526 Blake
Glenwood Springs, CO 81601

HONEYED ELK ROAST

Serves: 8
Prep Time: 5 hours

3-4 lbs. elk roast
  ½ cup burgundy wine
  1 tsp. monosodium glutamate
  2 tsp. salt
  2 tsp. pepper
  1 tsp. garlic powder
  6 thin lemon slices
  6 slices bacon

Sauce:
  ¼ cup butter
  ¼ cup honey
  ½ cup frozen orange juice concentrate
  ½ tsp. rosemary

Soak roast overnight in water with ½ cup vinegar. Remove from refrigerator, wash and dry. Splash on wine. Sprinkle on monosodium glutamate, salt, pepper and garlic powder. Place lemon slices on top of roast. Place bacon on top of lemon slices and secure with toothpicks. Place in 275 degree oven for five hours.

Melt butter in pan and add honey, orange juice and the remainder of wine. Add rosemary. Baste roast often with this honey sauce while baking.

Dion M. Luke
Ragged Mountain Outfitters, Inc.
1526 Blake
Glenwood Springs, CO 81601

SNOW ON THE MOUNTAIN

Serves: 6-8
Prep Time: 45 minutes

1½ lbs. ground elk
2 cups grated raw potatoes
⅔ cup chopped onion
1 clove garlic, minced
2 tsp. salt
½ tsp. pepper
¼ cup milk
2 eggs
¼ cup butter
3 cups water
2-3 tsp. cornstarch
2 cups sour cream
1 tsp. dill seeds
1 10 oz. package frozen peas, cooked

Combine first eight ingredients. Shape into 1½-inch balls and brown slowly in butter. Add ½ cup water, cover and simmer 20 minutes. Remove meatballs. Stir in flour, then remaining water. Simmer to thicken. Reduce heat, stir in sour cream and dill, add meatballs and peas. Heat but do not boil.

Dion M. Luke
Ragged Mountain Outfitters, Inc.
1526 Blake
Glenwood Springs, CO 81601

SWEET AND SOUR ELK

Serves: 4-6
Prep Time: 30-45 minutes

   3 **lbs. elk meat, diced into 1-inch cubes**
   ½ **cup cornstarch**
      salt and pepper
      cooking oil
   2 **medium onions, diced**
   1 **green pepper, diced**
   ¾ **cup sugar**
   1 **cup white vinegar**
   1 **cup soy sauce**
   2 **cups cooked rice**
   1 **cup pineapple chunks**
   ½ **cup pineapple juice**

Dip cubed elk in cornstarch seasoned with salt and pepper. Fry until golden brown. Drain. Place remaining ingredients in large pan and simmer until green pepper is tender. Add meat and cook until liquid is reduced to a thick sauce. Serve over rice.

Brenda Kuester
Rocky Point Outfitters
837 Swamp Creek Rd.
Plains, MT 59859

ELK MOUNTAIN ROAST

Serves: 6-8
Prep Time: 1 hour

3-4 lbs. elk roast	**salt and pepper**
1 slice bacon, cut into	**1 bay leaf**
small pieces	**2 cloves**
2 cloves garlic, crushed	**1 cup orange juice**

Cut slits in meat and insert small pieces of bacon and garlic. Salt and pepper well. Sear meat on all sides. Put meat in Dutch oven and place bay leaf and cloves on top. Baste with orange juice. Roast in 325 degree oven 25 minutes to the pound or until internal temperture is 170 degrees, basting frequently with orange juice.

Dion M. Luke
Ragged Mountain Outfitters, Inc.
1526 Blake
Glenwood Springs, CO 81601

MEATLOAF SANDWICHES

Serves: 10-12
Prep Time: 1½ hours

2 lbs. ground elk
1 lb. ground beef

1 cup water
1 pkg. Lipton onion soup mix

Mix all the above with hands until well blended. Shape into two loaves and bake uncovered in 9 x 13-inch pan for 1½ hours at 350 degrees. Let cool before slicing. Excellent served cold in buns with mustard and green pepper slices.

Linda Baumeister
Lone Wolf Guide Service
Box 631
Livingston, MT 59047

TERIYAKI CARIBOU

Serves: 4-6
Prep Time: 1½ hours

¼ cup soy sauce
3 T. brown sugar
½ cup water
1 tsp. ground ginger

1 tsp. garlic powder
¼ tsp. pepper
1-2 lbs. caribou

Slice caribou into ¼ to ½-inch strips. Mix all ingredients together, marinate caribou strips in sauce for one hour in a cool place. Remove from marinade, broil or pan fry.

Kathy
Arctic Rivers Guide Service
P.O. Box 124
Kotzebue, AK 99752

SHEEP CAMP STEAK

Serves: 6
Prep Time: 30 minutes

6 1-inch thick sheep steaks
½ cup coarsely chopped pecans
3 T. Worcestershire sauce
2 minced garlic cloves
¼ tsp. pepper
4 T. chopped parsley
3 T. oil
3 T. vinegar
½ tsp. thyme

In a bowl combine all ingredients except steak and pecans. In a deep platter score meat evenly. Cover steaks with sauce. Let stand one to two hours. Remove meat, pour sauce into a cup. Grease grill lightly. Cook steak seven minutes per side for a medium steak. Brush with sauce before you turn. Turn steak and brush with remaining sauce. Sprinkle with pecans. Grill until cooked as desired. Carefully remove to a platter. Let stand five minutes before serving.

Dixie Luke
Ragged Mountain Outfitters, Inc.
1526 Blake
Glenwood Springs, CO 81601

MINER'S SPRINGTIME BIGHORN

Serves: 6
Prep Time: 1½ hours

2½ cups sliced fresh rhubarb	¼ tsp. black pepper
¾ cup sugar	½ tsp. cinnamon
¾ cup water	¼ tsp. nutmeg
¼ cup butter	1 cup parsley
1 lb. trimmed sheep meat, cut into 1-inch cubes	1 T. cornstarch
1 tsp. salt	2 cups cooked rice

Place rhubarb in bowl, stir in sugar and water, set aside for 30 minutes. Drain, reserving syrup. In skillet, melt butter, saute meat, onion and seasoning until meat is browned on all sides. Stir in parsley and saute a few more minutes. Stir in rhubarb syrup. Simmer gently, covered for 40 minutes. Stir in drained rhubarb. Continue simmering, covered, for 20 to 30 minutes or until meat is tender. Combine cornstarch and 1 T. water. Stir into meat mixture, cook gently two to three minutes longer until meat mixture is thickened. Serve over hot cooked rice.

Dixie Luke
Ragged Mountain Outfitters, Inc.
1526 Blake
Glenwood Springs, CO 81601

LION SUPREME

Serves: 8
Prep Time: 1 hour 45 minutes

- **1 lion hindquarter or 8 steaks**
- **½ cup margarine**
- **½ tsp. salt**
- **1 tsp. garlic salt**
- **2 T. dried, minced onion**
- **wine**

Put meat in casserole dish and pour ½ cup margarine over. Add salt, garlic salt and onion. Bake one hour at 350 degrees. Remove from oven, marinate for 45 minutes in wine. If meat is tough, the wine will tenderize it.

Jane Smith
5/S Ranch
Star Rt., Box 282
Trout Creek, MT 59874

MOUNTAIN LION STEW IN BEER

Serves: 4
Prep Time: 2 hours

1 lb. lion meat, cut into 1-inch pieces
3 T. flour
1 tsp. salt
1/8 tsp. pepper
1 garlic clove, minced
2 T. cooking fat
1 12oz. can beer

1 small bay leaf
1 cup carrots, sliced diagonally
1¼ lbs. yellow onions, sliced ¼-inch thick
2 T. butter
½ cup water
2 T. snipped parsley

Combine flour, salt and pepper. Dredge lion. Reserve excess flour. Brown meat and garlic in cooking fat in Dutch oven. Pour off drippings. Add beer and bay leaf, stirring to combine. Cover tightly and cook slowly 1½ hours. Remove the bay leaf. Add carrots and continue cooking, covered, for 30 minutes. Meanwhile, cook onions in butter in frying pan over medium-high heat for 15 minutes, stirring occasionally. Add onions to meat mixture and continue cooking 10 minutes, covered, or until meat is tender. Combine reserved flour and water, gradually stir into cooking liquid and cook until thickened, about five minutes. Stir in parsley. Serve with bannock.

Dion M. Luke
Ragged Mountain Outfitters, Inc.
1526 Blake
Glenwood Springs, CO 81601

ANTELOPE ENCHILADAS

Serves: 4-6
Prep Time: 1½ hours

**2-3 lbs. ground antelope, mixed with 10 percent
    beef tallow
  1 onion, chopped
1½ lbs. colby cheese, grated
  1 can pitted black olives
  1 package dry taco seasoning
  2 tsp. black pepper
12 large flour tortillas
  1 small head lettuce, shredded
  2 tomatoes, diced
  2 tsp. cumin
  2 cans mild enchilada sauce**

Brown meat. Add taco seasoning, cumin and pepper. Simmer on low heat for five minutes to extract flavor from spices, add a little water if the mixture becomes dry. Place about ½ cup meat mixture on a tortilla, sprinkle with 2 T. grated cheese and 1 T. olives. Roll up tortilla and place seam down in a greased baking dish. Continue the same procedure with the remaining tortillas using all of the meat. Top with enchilada sauce, remaining cheese and onion. Refrigerate until ½ hour before serving or bake immediately at 350 degrees for ½ hour. Serve topped with lettuce, tomatoes and olives. These enchiladas are good made with buffalo or deer meat also. The beef tallow makes a big difference in the flavor.

Mary Beth Kibler
Myron Kibler's Outfitting and Guide Service
Box A-6
Sand Springs, MT 59077

GRANNY BUTLER'S ANTELOPE STEAK

Serves: 4
Prep Time: 30 minutes

1½ lbs. antelope steak, each about ½-inch thick
¾ cup flour
1 tsp. salt
1 tsp. pepper
1 tsp. garlic powder
1 egg
1 cup milk
½ cup cooking oil

With a meat tenderizer, pound steak on both sides. Combine milk and egg in a bowl. On a plate, mix flour, salt, pepper and garlic powder. Dip antelope steaks in milk and then dredge in flour mixture. In a large cast iron skillet on medium-high heat add enough oil and cook on both sides. Add more oil for remainder of steaks. Serve with mashed potatoes and carrots. Gravy can be made from skillet drippings if desired.

Kay Butler
Ragged Mountain Outfitters, Inc.
1526 Blake
Glenwood Springs, CO 81601

BAKED BEAR STEW

Serves: 6
Prep Time: 2½ hours

3	lbs. bear stew meat	⅓	cup salad oil
2	cups onion, minced	½	cup unsifted flour
2	cloves garlic, minced	¾	cup red cooking wine
2	bay leaves	2	cups water
1½	tsp. salt	6	oz. tomato paste
1½	tsp. monosodium		cooked noodles
	glutamate		
¼	tsp. pepper		

Place bear meat, onion, garlic and bay leaves in shallow baking pan. Sprinkle with a mixture of salt, monosodium glutamate and pepper. Bake uncovered in a 425 degree oven for 10 minutes. Reduce heat to 300 degrees and continue baking for 30 minutes.

Make sauce of flour, salad oil, red cooking wine, water and tomato paste. Cook until smooth. Pour over meat, cover and bake in a 300 degree oven about one to 1½ hours or until meat is very tender but not dry. Serve over hot noodles.

Dion M. Luke
Ragged Mountain Outfitters, Inc.
1526 Blake
Glenwood Springs, CO 81601

SWISSED BUFFALO STEAK

Serves: 4
Prep Time: 1½ hours

2 lbs. buffalo steak
1 can mushroom soup
2 cups tomato juice
¼ cup chopped onion
¼ cup chopped celery
⅛ cup chopped green pepper
1 cup flour
1 tsp. salt
1 tsp. pepper
½ tsp. garlic salt
½ tsp. red pepper
½ cup vegetable oil

Pound meat to tenderize. Sift together flour, red pepper, garlic salt, pepper and salt. Heat oil in skillet. Coat each steak in flour mixture and brown in hot oil. Place in a baking dish. Combine mushroom soup, tomato sauce, onion, celery and green pepper and pour over steak. Bake for one to 1½ hours at 325 to 350 degrees.

Mary Beth Kibler
Myron Kibler's Outfitting and Guide Service
Box A-6
Sand Springs, MT 59077

BAKED HEART WITH RICE SALAD

Serves: 8
Prep Time: 1½ hours

1 heart	Sauce:
1 can bean sprouts, rinsed and drained	2 slices bacon
1 cup unpeeled cucumbers	1 cup mayonnaise
1 cup radishes	2 T. soy sauce
1 cup celery	salt and pepper
1 can red kidney beans	
2½ cups cooked rice	
3-6 hard boiled eggs	

Bake heart for one hour in water, then dice up the whole heart. Dice and slice eggs, celery, radishes, cucumbers. Layer with bean sprouts, kidney beans. Toss with rice.

Sauce: fry bacon until crisp. Crumble into salad. Reserve grease, mix with one cup mayonnaise and 2 T. soy sauce, salt and pepper. Toss gently into salad so it is mixed thoroughly. Garnish with paprika.

Betsy Henry
High Country Outfitters
Box 26
Joseph, OR 97846

HEART SANDWICH MEAT

Serves: 8-10
Prep Time: 2 hours

1 deer or elk heart	½ tsp. thyme
1 small clove garlic	½ tsp. salt
1 bay leaf	¼ tsp. pepper
½ tsp. basil	water to cover

In a two-quart saucepan with a lid, put the elk or deer heart plus all the above ingredients. Cover heart with water and simmer about two hours (until tender). Cool, then slice for sandwiches.

Note: You can substitute grouse for the heart.

Ann Barker
JJJ Wilderness Ranch
Box 310
Augusta, MT 59410

ELK CAMP LIVER APPETIZER

Serves: 4-8
Prep Time: 25 minutes

> **allow ½ lb. liver per person**
> **½ to 1 lb. bacon**
> **½ onion per person**
> **flour, to dust**
> **salt and pepper**

Cook bacon until crisp, retain grease. Slice onions and cube. Cook in bacon grease until tender. Slice liver ½-inch thick, salt and pepper. Shake in a paper bag with flour. Fry liver in retained bacon grease until brown (add more grease if necessary). Do not overcook. Liver should be on rare side. Serve with bacon and onions.

Dick "Dead Eye" Jones
Ragged Mountain Outfitters, Inc.
1526 Blake
Glenwood Springs, CO 81601

DOVE-WILD RICE CASSEROLE

Serves: 6
Prep Time: 20 minutes

   1 **cube chicken bouillon**
   1 **cup hot water**
   1 **cup celery, chopped**
   1 **tsp. celery salt**
   1 **tsp. onion salt**
   1/8 **tsp. pepper**
   1 **T. parsley, minced**
   1 **T. soy sauce**
   1 **cup white rice, cooked**
   1/4 **cup wild rice, cooked**
   2 **T. butter**
   8 **doves or 2 pheasants**

Dissolve bouillon in hot water; add celery and parboil. Add
seasonings, rice and butter. Place skinned birds in a
greased casserole; cover with rice. Bake at 350 degrees for
three hours or until tender.

Ruth Taggart
P & R Hunting Lodge
Rt. 5, Box 117
Dallas, SD 57529

SAGE GROUSE APPETIZERS

Serves: 4
Prep Time: ½ hour

**2 sage grouse breasts,
    boned and fileted into
    thin slices
1 egg, beaten
½ cup canned milk
1½ cups flour**

**½ tsp. salt
fresh ground pepper
pinch of sage
oil**

Heat an inch or so of oil in a pot or skillet. Mix egg and
milk together. In another dish, mix flour and seasonings
together. Dip slices of breast in egg mixture, then in flour
and fry quickly in hot oil, just until golden brown. Be sure
you get a head start on these — your crew and hunters will
eat them faster than you can turn them out!

Coralee McKee
Boulder Lake Lodge
Box 1100
Pinedale, WY 82941

SMOKED PHEASANT

Serves: 6
Prep Time: 14 hours

½ cup liquid smoke
1 cup Morton's tender-quick salt
½ cup coarse pickling salt
1 gal. or more water

Combine all ingredients until dissolved. Soak 12 hours completely covered in plastic container in refrigerator. Wash in clean water and cover with heavy foil in roaster, and bake according to size or 1½ hours at 350 degrees. Let sit ½ hour before slicing. Recipe is enough for two pheasants.

SOUTH DAKOTA PHEASANT IN SOUR CREAM

Serves: 3-4
Prep Time: 15 minutes

1 pheasant, cut into   ½ tsp. pepper
   serving pieces   fat
½ cup flour   1 green pepper, chopped
1 tsp. salt   1 cup sour cream

Dip pheasant in flour, salt and pepper; brown in hot fat until golden. Cover and cook slowly for 30 minutes. Add green pepper and sour cream; cook over very low heat until cream is just hot.

Ruth Taggart
P & R Hunting Lodge
Rt. 5, Box 117
Dallas, SD 57529

BARBEQUED MONTANA GAME BIRDS

Serves: 4-6
Prep Time: 1½ hours

3-4 lbs. game birds	2 tsp. salt
3 cups tomato juice	4 tsp. mustard
1 T. sugar	3 T. Worcestershire
½ cup vinegar	1 tsp. pepper
½ cup catsup	1 onion, sliced

Cut up birds, brown in skillet in oil and place in a baking dish. Combine the above ingredients and pour over meat. Bake at 325 to 350 degrees for approximately one hour. A longer baking time and lower baking temperature makes meat more tender.

Mary Beth Kibler
Myron Kibler's Outfitting and Guide Service
Box A-6
Sand Springs, MT 59077

COLORADO BANNOCK

Serves: 4
Prep Time: 30 minutes

2 cups flour
2 tsp. baking soda
2 T. dried milk
4 T. bacon fat
½ cup raisins (optional)

1 tsp. salt
2 T. sugar
enough water to make
soft dough

Mix all ingredients with water to make a soft dough.
Grease a cast iron skillet and put on medium-high heat.
Place ⅓ of soft dough in skillet and flatten with a fork or
turner. Brown on both sides being sure the inside is well-
cooked. For sweet bannock and added nourishment while
out camping, add raisins to the dough while mixing.

SOUR MILK BISCUITS

Serves: 6-8
Prep Time: 30 minutes

2 cups flour
2 tsp. baking powder
2 T. lard

1 tsp. salt
¼ tsp. soda
1 cup sour milk

Sift dry ingredients into mixing bowl, rub in lard with fin-
ger tips. Add sour milk. Mix into a soft and spongy dough.
Roll ½-inch thick and cut biscuits. Lightly flour shallow
pan or cookie sheet, place biscuits not too close together
and bake 12 minutes at 350 degrees.

Dion M. Luke
Ragged Mountain Outfitters, Inc.
1526 Blake
Glenwood Springs, CO 81601

MEAT MARINADE

Serves: 4
Prep Time: 15 minutes

1½ **lbs. boneless meat (chunks for shish-ka-bob, chops or steaks**
1 **tsp. garlic salt**
¼ **tsp. freshly ground pepper**
½ **tsp. dry mustard**

½ **tsp. chili powder**
1 **tsp. minced onion**
¼ **cup cider vinegar**
2 **T. catsup**
2 **T. oil**

Prepare meat (trim or cut up) and set aside. Mix all remaining ingredients well with a wire wisk. Coat pieces of meat with marinade and place in a shallow pan. Pour remaining marinade over meat, cover and refrigerate for several hours. Broil, using marinade to baste. This works well with elk, moose, venison or antelope meat.

Coralee McKee
Boulder Lake Lodge
Box 1100
Pinedale, WY 82941

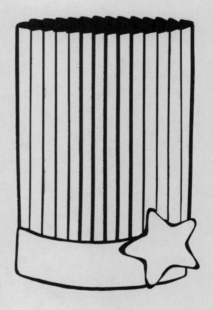

CELEBRITY
CHEFS

Chuck Saunders
President
Saunders Archery Co.

Chuck Saunders founded the Saunders Archery Company in 1941. The company specializes in archery accessories and sling-shots and is now the largest in the world in these two areas. Many of their products are patented and they have received 39 patents in these two fields besides having eight now pend-ing. The company was also active in founding the Bowhunters Who Care organization.

VENISON CASSEROLE

Serves: 2-4
Prep Time: 45 minutes

½ pkg. egg noodles
1 lb. ground venison
½ lb. pork sausage
1 T. green pepper, chopped
1 medium onion, chopped thickly
1 can tomato soup
1 can corn
1 can mushrooms
1 can tomato sauce
 salt and pepper
¼ tsp. garlic powder
 pinch oregano

Boil noodles until tender in salted water and drain. Saute crumbled meat, green pepper and onion in small amount of fat. Add other ingredients. Put noodles in greased casserole dish and then pour other mixture into noodles. Bake for about 30 minutes in 275 degree oven.

Chuck Saunders
Columbus, Nebraska

Steve McCarthy
President
Michael's of Oregon

"The trouble with running a busy hunting accessory company," says Michael's of Oregon President Steve McCarthy, "is finding time to get out hunting." But as busy as he is, managing factories in Portland, Oregon and Boise, Idaho, Steve does carve out some time to hunt ducks and geese on the Oregon Coast, and both elk and pheasant in Idaho.

Steve's company employs about 125 people making sling swivels, leather and nylon slings, SIDEKICK® nylon holsters and accessories, scope covers and almost every conceivable accessory for black powder shooters. In a nutshell, Steve believes in making everything "Uncle Mike's" sells in their own factories, doing a quality job and constantly improving every product in the line. Steve cut through a lot of legal mumbo-jumbo and wrote his own product warranty: Satisfaction guaranteed or your money back . . . period.

BAY DUCKS

duck breasts
peanut, almond or Wesson oil
thyme
pepper
brandy

Use absolutely fresh ducks. Skin, remove breasts from bone. Remove liver, clean and trim. Use remainder of bird for a stock or discard. Drain breast meat, dry between paper towels. Sprinkle with fresh chopped thyme and fresh ground pepper. Heat heavy iron pan. When hot, add oil. When oil and pan are hot, but not smoking, sear breasts for two to five minutes per side, depending on their thickness. Remove to a hot platter. Meat should be rare inside, brown outside. Fry the duck liver the same way. Deglaze the pan with brandy. Serve warm platter with breasts, livers, sauce from pan. Surround with sprigs of parsley. Rice and buttered carrots are good with this dish.

Steve McCarthy
Portland, Oregon

Ron Gangelhoff
Chairman
Chicago Cutlery Co.

Ron Gangelhoff is chairman of Chicago Cutlery Company, and is a businessman and an outdoorsman. Prior to joining Chicago Cutlery, he had many years experience as a fishing guide and resort owner in northern Minnesota. In both business and pleasure, Ron is committed to educating sportsmen about how quality sporting knives can enhance the outdoor experience.

Chicago Cutlery manufactures a full line of quality sporting cutlery including pocketknives, fillet and skinning knives, ergonomically-designed hunting and fishing knives and sharpening tools. The blades are handcrafted from high-carbon stainless steel and are hand-ground to a sharp edge.

Chicago Cutlery has been a leader in the commercial cutlery industry for more than 50 years and entered the sporting market in 1979.

DUCK ON A GRILL

Serves: 2
Prep Time: 1 hour

- ½ **cup onion, chopped**
- 1 **stick margarine, melted**
- 3 **boned duck breasts, sliced in finger-length slivers**
- 2 **24 x 18-inch pieces heavy duty foil**

Sprinkle chopped onion on foil. Lay slices of duck on foil and pour melted margarine over duck. (Butter may be used.) Take all four corners of foil and gather, leaving a small opening at top. Cook ½ hour on gas grill on high heat. Open and stir with spoon. Cook for another 30 minutes, but not longer than one hour 10 minutes.

Ron Gangelhoff
Minneapolis, Minnesota

Marvin E. Epling
President and General Manager
Crosman Airguns

Marvin E. Epling is president and general manager of Crosman Airguns in Fairport, New York, and a vice president of the parent Coleman Company.

Epling is a career Coleman employee. As president and general manager of Crosman Airguns, he is in charge of the manufacturing and marketing of Crosman pneumatic and CO_2 airguns, Golden Eagle archery equipment and Ranging optical rangefinders for hunting and commercial applications.

He came to Coleman in 1970 and worked for Coleman's Camping Trailer Division before joining Crosman in 1971 as the regional sales manager for the West Coast, In 1975, he was promoted to sales and marketing vice president for Crosman and in 1980 to his present position.

ANTELOPE STROGANOFF

Serves: 6-8
Prep Time: 30 minutes

2 lbs. antelope, boned	½ tsp. pepper
4 T. butter	1 T. horseradish
1 cup onions, minced	1 can mushroom soup
½ lb. mushrooms	1 cup water
3 T. flour	1½ cups sour cream
½ tsp. salt	½ cup white chablis

Cut antelope into 1½-inch wide and 2-inch long strips.
Salt, pepper and flour meat pieces. In an electric skillet
melt margarine. Brown onions and meat. Mix soup and
water together. Pour over meat, stir. Add mushrooms,
horseradish and wine. Cook over low to medium heat until
meat is tender. Test before serving. Stir in sour cream.
Serve over rice or noodles. Serve with wine-glazed carrots,
tossed salad and rolls.

WINE GLAZED CARROTS

Serves: 6

carrots, (enough for six servings)
1 T. butter
2 T. light muscat wine

Peel carrots and slice lengthwise. Cook in salted water
until just tender. Drain and saute in 1 T. butter until
lightly browned. Add muscat and simmer until wine has
evaporated.

Marvin Epling
Middlesex, New York

Ron Lawrence
Vice-President of Sales
Golden Eagle Archery

Ron has a broad sporting goods background. He started in the business over 12 years ago as a distributor/salesman, and always carried a fishing rod, a shotgun and a rifle in the trunk. For a time, he was sales manager for a sporting goods distributor, then became the northwest regional manager for Crosman Airguns, a division of Coleman. This move allowed him to fish and hunt in Oregon, Idaho, Washington, Montana and Alaska. In 1983, Ron became the vice-president of sales for Golden Eagle Archery, another Coleman division.

His hobbies include hunting, fishing, skiing and cooking. Ron says, "You don't get a body like this from not eating." It is a little known fact, but as a cook and canner of wild game, he has won sixteen blue ribbons, a Ball Jar Canning Award and a second place ribbon at a county fair.

THE BEST VENISON JERKY

Serves: varies
Prep Time: 24 hours

- **½ venison ham well trimmed**
- **⅓ cup sugar**
- **⅓ cup non-iodized salt**
- **2 cups soy sauce**
- **1 cup water**
- **1 cup apple wine (red or white)**
- **½ tsp. garlic salt**
- **½ tsp. onion salt**
- **1 T. coarse ground pepper**
- **1 tsp. liquid smoke**

Slice meat with the grain in ¼- to ½-inch slices. Reserve
pepper except for ½ tsp. Combine all ingredients, including the ½ tsp. pepper, in a large glass or plastic container.
Mix well. Add meat to mixture and let stand for eight to
10 hours. After meat has marinated, remove from container to dry. Spread paper towels over newspapers and lay
meat slices on the towels. Use remaining pepper, or pepper
to your taste. Allow to air dry for eight hours. Next, being
careful not to lose too much pepper, lay meat on oven
grates. Allow meat to dry at 150 degrees for four to eight
hours. Check every couple of hours.

Ron Lawrence
Creswell, Oregon

Robert Beeman
President
Beeman Precision Arms, Inc.

Dr. Robert Beeman and his wife, Toshiko, began selling precision adult airguns from their home in 1972. Their company, Beeman Precision Arms, is now the largest distributor of Europe's adult airguns in the U.S. In addition, the company now distributes a variety of fine, European firearms as well. Beeman is a leading authority on airguns and has one of the world's finest collections of antique airguns. In the photo, Beeman is holding one of his favorite specimens, a .58 caliber pneumatic rifle made by Bate in England in the 1800s. The recipe Beeman contributes reflects his taste for the type of "small game" one can hunt with an airgun!

FROG LEGS IN CREAM

Serves: varies
Prep Time: 45 minutes

frog legs   **salt and pepper**
flour   **half & half**
butter

Soak legs in salt water about 15 minutes. Drain and rinse
well. Roll in flour and brown in butter. Season with salt
and pepper. Cover and cook slowly on top of stove for about
20 minutes or until tender. (Time depends on size of legs.)
Remove cover, pour half & half over legs. Cook slowly a few
minutes. A little more salt and pepper may be needed. If
sauce is too thin, thicken with flour and water. Delicious
served over noodles or rice.

Robert Beeman
San Rafael, California

Robert Hoague
President
Camo Clan Corp.

A bowhunter since 1948, Robert Hoague is the founder of The Camo Clan, the unique mail-order company that features exclusive clothing designs made for bowhunters. He has been responsible for the creation of Snow Camo and Tree Stand Camo as well as the recoloring of the Jungle Camo prints to blend in with North American hunting conditions.

A ready volunteer for camp cook since his teens, Robert enjoys wild game cooking and has a variety of recipes specializing in the preparation of venison, rabbit, squirrel and antelope.

DEER BEER CHILI

Serves: 8-12

1	2-inch strip of bacon	2	tomatoes
4	cups cubed venison	1	large bell pepper
1	bay leaf	½	tsp. brown sugar
1	large can tomato paste	2	cans kidney beans
2	large cans tomato sauce	3-4	cans beer
1	large onion		salt and pepper
1	large jar chili powder		

Soak beans overnight and rinse thoroughly. Put venison cubes in large pot with bacon, salt and pepper. Stir frequently until meat is browned. Remove bacon and add tomato sauce. Spoon in as much chili pepper as you can handle, stir. Raise the heat to medium and cover for four minutes. Dice the onion and pepper. Peel the tomatoes and cut into chunks. Save the seeds and juices from all vegetables. Discard the tomato skins and pepper stems. Add onion, peppers, tomatoes, beans, seeds and juices, tomato paste, bay leaf and sugar. Do not saute the vegetables before adding them to the meat. Stir all ingredients. Add two cans of beer and stir. Cover and heat, stirring occasionally. Once the chili comes to a slow boil, reduce heat to low. Stir and cover for 15 minutes. Taste and add more seasonings to taste. Add beer if it looks too thick. Cover and heat on low for two to four hours. Stir hourly. Raise heat to medium five minutes before serving.

Robert Hoague
Dallas, Texas

David Forbes
President
Hunter's Specialties

Dave, being an avid out-
doorsman, has always
strived to improve the
quality of hunting and
hunting equipment for
all. He is deeply com-
mitted to wildlife habi-
tat preservation and its
growth. He feels the
mood of the nation is to
protect, preserve and
improve what we have
taken for granted for so
long.

Along with Hunter's
Specialties' staff, Dave
strives for innovating
new products and insists on the highest standards of
quality for all products.

DUCK SUPREME

Serves: 4
Prep Time: 6 hours

6 duck breasts, fillet each breast in half
   milk
   flour
   salt and pepper
   butter
½ cup wine or sherry (or to taste)

Pound each duck breast with meat mallet to tenderize. Cover with milk and refrigerate four to six hours or overnight. Dredge in flour, salt and pepper. Brown in butter over moderate heat. Add enough water to cover ¾ of the meat. Sprinkle wine or sherry over the top. Put lid on pan and simmer 45 minutes to one hour. Liquid will thicken to gravy. You may need to add water while cooking. Serve by itself or over rice or noodles.

David Forbes
Cedar Rapids, Iowa

J. Michael Murray
President and General Manager
Ranging Inc.

J. Michael Murray is president and general manager for Ranging , Inc., a position he has held since 1971. Located in Fairport, New York, Ranging was founded in 1966 and manufactures optical rangefinders for outdoor, sport, professional and industrial use. In 1984,Ranging was purchased by the Coleman Company.

Murray, a former Marine, attended Syracuse and Fairfield Universities in New York. From 1969-70 he served as president of Crosman Arms. Mike is on the board of directors of the National Bowhunter Education Foundation and on the executive committee for the International Bowhunting Organization.

OLE SETTLERS VENISON STEAKS

Serves: 6
Prep Time: 1 hour

- **6 venison steaks cut ¾-inch thick**
- **6 slices bacon**
- **2 T. flour**
- **1 tsp. celery salt**
  dash of thyme, sage, cayenne
- **1 cup red wine**
- **1 cup white vinegar**
- **1 T. sugar**
- **4 T. butter**
- **4 white onions**

Slice onions into 1-inch slices and soak in vinegar and sugar for an hour. Saute onions in 2 T. butter until translucent. Remove onions but save pan drippings. While onions are sauteeing, remove fat and gristle from steaks. Wrap bacon around steaks and secure with toothpicks. Mix together flour and spices. Roll steaks and bacon in flour and spices and fry in remaining butter over hot flame for three minutes on one side, five minutes on the other. Remove steaks when done to warm platter. Finally, add red wine to frying pan, stirring mixture to dissolve all juices. Simmer until sauce thickens slightly, then pour over meat. Serve onions over steaks.

J. Michael Murray
Rochester, New York

Andy Simo
President
New Archery Products

Andy Simo, president of
New Archery Products,
manufactures the well-
known Razorbak &
Thunderhead Broad-
heads. A native of
Czechoslovakia, he
grew up eating home
grown vegetables, home
butchered meat and
wild game of all kinds.
Hunting was a means of
feeding the family as
well as a traditional
well-respected sport
spanning back several
generations.

Svickova is a midly pickled meat dish that may be used
with beef as well. Recipe is somewhat involved, but well
worth the effort.

SVICKOVA VENISON

Serves: 4-6
Prep Time: 8 days

1 3-4 lb. venison roast	8-10 whole peppercorns
8-10 garlic cloves	2 bay leaves
2-3 ribs celery, chunked	salt to taste
1 large onion, chunked	3-4 T. vinegar
3 carrots, chunked	1 large onion, chunked

Trim all surface membrane and fat from roast and rinse
well. Make slits in top of meat and insert garlic cloves.
Bring vegetables and spices to a boil in two quarts of
water and simmer until crisp. Let cool. Add salt and vinegar and mix well. Place meat in non-aluminum container.
Pour water mixture with vegetables over meat, adding
water until meat is covered. Let meat marinate in cool
place for seven to eight days turning roast over each day.
Bring meat/marinade to a boil on stove and turn down to
simmer. Skim foam off as it rises from meat. Simmer approximately 10 minutes. Remove meat from mixture and
place in roaster. Add one large onion, chunked, around
meat. Roast 1½ to 2 hours at 325 degrees or until done.

To make gravy, remove vegetables to separate pan and
mash. Add approximately one quart of water mixture.
Bring to a simmer. Mix ½ cup flour with water and add to
vegetable mixture to thicken. Strain mixture. Adjust
seasoning to taste adding 1 tsp. sugar and 1 or 2 tsp. of
vinegar. Add Half & Half or milk to taste. Slice and serve
gravy over meat or add sliced meat to bowl of gravy.

Andy Simo
Berwyn, Illinois

George Schneider
Owner, Chairman of the Board
La Crosse Rubber Mills

George is principal owner and chairman of the board of La Crosse Rubber Mills, Inc. Founded in 1897, La Crosse Rubber Mills is one of the oldest and the largest manufacturers of rubber footwear in the country. The product line includes over 200 different styles of sporting, industrial, farm and work boots.

Sporting boots, such as the insulated chest wader, hip waders and the leather top/rubber bottom pacs are becoming an ever increasing and important part of the business. George says "Our job is to keep the sportsman's feet warm, dry and comfortable and that's what we will do."

Rice Lake, Wisconsin, was George's original home. He now lives in Redondo Beach, California, where he is also chairman of the Bay Cities National Bank. One of his favorite business philosophies is "You make money with people, not on them". He spends his spare time swimming, traveling and enjoying the great outdoors.

FISCH GASTHOF SCHNEIDER

Serves: 8
Prep Time: 6½ hours

8 trout (or any type fish sufficient)
Marinade:

1 cup white wine	¼ tsp. garlic, minced
⅛ cup olive oil	juice of one lemon
½ tsp. dillweed	1-2 onions, thinly sliced
¼ tsp. celery seed	4-8 slices bacon

Mix marinade sauce of wine, olive oil, lemon juice and seasonings. Place fish in open pan and pour sauce over fish. Place sliced onions on top of fish. During three to six hours of marinating, baste fish occasionally with sauce. Make aluminum foil boat large enough to hold all fish on barbeque grill. Coat bottom of foil with grease or spray with Pam to keep fish from sticking to foil. Place fish in boat and cover with sauce. Place sliced onions on top of fish and slices of bacon on top of onion. Cover fish with foil to preserve moisture. Take fork and jab several holes in cover of fish boat. Cook approximately ½ hour, depending on size of fish and temperature of fire.

George W. Schneider
Redondo Beach, California

CAMP COOKING

The annual NAHC Wild Game Cookbook is becoming a real tradition—an important way for members to share the enjoyment of hunting.

A special edition of our cookbook is being planned—one that will feature camp cooking, tasty recipes to be used from the elk camps of British Columbia to the turkey camps of the South.

To make this cookbook the very best possible, we're asking that you share those recipes which have become a part of your hunting camp tradition. As in the past, we'll emphasize recipes with wild game as the main ingredient but we also plan to include a wide variety of recipes which will add to the pleasure of your hunt:

- Meals which can be assembled at home for ease of preparation in camp
- Trail foods to stick in your pocket
- Breakfasts—great ways to start off the day
- Hearty dinners
- Camp stove specialties
- Cooking over an open fire

So send us your recipe! Share your experience and enjoyment with other members in this special upcoming edition of the NAHC Wild Game Cookbook.

SEND US YOUR GAME RECIPE

Title: _____

Serves: _____

Prep Time: _____

Ingredients:

_____
_____
_____
_____
_____
_____
_____
_____
_____

Directions:

_____ fold here
_____
_____
_____
_____
_____
_____
_____
_____
_____
_____
_____
_____
_____
_____
_____
_____
_____
_____
_____
_____

Your NAHC Member # _____

Your Name _____

Address _____

City/State/Zip _____

North American Hunting Club
P. O. Box 35557
Minneapolis, MN 55435

(tape or staple here)

Hunters belong in the NAHC...
and it's so *simple* to join!
Cut out and mail one of the cards below.

Count me in...
I want to increase my hunting pleasure and skill.
Here's my $18 annual dues for membership in the North American Hunting Club Inc. I understand my membership will start immediately upon receipt of this application and continue for 12 months.

RECOMMENDED BY

Name _____

NAHC MEMBER # _____

Name _____

Address _____

City_____ State_____ Zip _____

Type of Hunter: ☐ Firearms ☐ Archery ☐ Handgun ☐ Muzzleloader

Check Game Hunted: ☐ Big Game ☐ Small Game ☐ Waterfowl ☐ Upland Birds

Check One:

☐ Check enclosed
☐ Bill my MasterCard
☐ Bill my VISA
☐ Bill me later

Credit Card No. _____ Exp. Date _____

Signature _____

Count me in...
I want to increase my hunting pleasure and skill.
Here's my $18 annual dues for membership in the North American Hunting Club Inc. I understand my membership will start immediately upon receipt of this application and continue for 12 months.

RECOMMENDED BY

Name _____

NAHC MEMBER # _____

Name _____

Address _____

City_____ State_____ Zip _____

Type of Hunter: ☐ Firearms ☐ Archery ☐ Handgun ☐ Muzzleloader

Check Game Hunted: ☐ Big Game ☐ Small Game ☐ Waterfowl ☐ Upland Birds

Check One:

☐ Check enclosed
☐ Bill my MasterCard
☐ Bill my VISA
☐ Bill me later

Credit Card No. _____ Exp. Date _____

Signature _____

BUSINESS REPLY CARD
FIRST CLASS   PERMIT NO. 17619   MPLS., MN

POSTAGE WILL BE PAID BY ADDRESSEE

North American Hunting Club, Inc.
P.O. Box 35557
Minneapolis, Minn. 55435

NO POSTAGE
NECESSARY
IF MAILED
IN THE
UNITED STATES

BUSINESS REPLY CARD
FIRST CLASS   PERMIT NO. 17619   MPLS., MN

POSTAGE WILL BE PAID BY ADDRESSEE

North American Hunting Club, Inc.
P.O. Box 35557
Minneapolis, Minn. 55435

NO POSTAGE
NECESSARY
IF MAILED
IN THE
UNITED STATES